TILES

1,000 YEARS OF ARCHITECTURAL DECORATION

TILES

1,000 YEARS OF ARCHITECTURAL DECORATION

HANS VAN LEMMEN

HARRY N. ABRAMS, INC., PUBLISHERS

FRONTISPIECE: Tiles of *circa* 1730 in the Salao Nobre of the Palácio dos Condes de Anadia, Mangualde, near Viseu, Portugal.

PAGE SIX: An innovative and colourful panel showing the whole of the 1992 Arcana range of tiles, designed by the Venetian artist, Nino Nemo.

PAGE EIGHT: View from the Arab Hall towards the staircase at Leighton House, London. The plain turquoise tiles on the staircase were made by William De Morgan. Those on the left are sixteenth- and seventeenth-century Islamic Iznik tiles.

PAGE TEN: The Portland Building, head-quarters of the Municipal Government of Portland, Oregon, designed by Michael Graves in 1989. The exterior is covered with tiles from the Combi-Colour range by Gail-Inax AG of Germany.

Designed by Sara Robin
Picture Research by Susan Bolsom-Morris

Library of Congress Cataloging-in-Publication Data

Lemmen, Hans van.
Tiles: 1000 years of architectural decoration/by Hans van Lemmen, with a contribution by Susan Tunick.
p.   cm.
Includes bibliographical references and index.
ISBN 0–8109–3867–7
1. Tiles.   2. Decoration and ornament, Architectural. I. Tunick, Susan.   II. Title.
NA3705.L46 1993
721'.0443—dc20   93–7308
CIP

Published in 1993 by Harry N. Abrams, Incorporated, New York
A Times Mirror Company
All rights reserved. No part of the contents of this book may be reproduced without the written permission of the publisher

This book was designed and produced by
Calmann & King Ltd., London
Printed and bound in Singapore

For Ken Beaulah

CONTENTS

Acknowledgements   5

Introduction   11

1 FOR GOD AND EARTHLY PRINCES   15

2 PAINTED MAGNIFICENCE   41

3 THE MARCH OF THE MACHINE   95

4 THE TRIUMPH OF THE DESIGNER   135

5 THE NEW WORLD by Susan Tunick   167

6 THE MODERN AGE   199

Bibliography   234

Picture Credits   236

Index   237

INTRODUCTION

Tiles have been a part of European architecture ever since the first buildings of brick and stone were erected, and are an important part of our visual heritage. The different techniques by which tiles have been made, the great variety of uses to which they have been put, and the wealth of ways in which they have been decorated make up a fascinating and intriguing history.

Firstly the word 'tile' itself needs definition. It is derived from the Latin noun *'tegula'*, from the verb *'tegere'*, which means 'to cover', although in Roman times the word *'tegula'* at first referred to roof tiles. Generally speaking, however, and in the context of this book, tiles are defined as flat pieces of fired clay, used on the floors and walls of buildings. They are often glazed, which renders their surfaces impervious to water, and allows colour and many different types of imagery and pattern to be used in their decoration.

The use of tiles in architecture has been governed by both their decorative and practical appeal. Tiling provides a surface that is hygienic, easy to clean and waterproof. It is fire retardant, but can also help radiate heat. The decoration of tiles has been equally diverse, with single images, entire scenes, or emblematic devices finding favour for reasons that have encompassed the didactic and moral as well as the symbolic. The appreciation of tiles simply for their aesthetic effect has also been important, as patterns, textures and coloured glazes have always exerted a strong visual attraction.

Tiles may be of any shape, but one fact that they all have in common is that they are applied to a surface (which is usually flat, but may occasionally be curved), and thus can be removed without affecting the structure of a building. This makes tiles different from other architectural ceramics, such as glazed bricks, unglazed terracotta or glazed faience building blocks, which, when in place, are an integral part of the building, and cannot easily be removed. Tiles are essentially more two-dimensional in their use and effect, although strict separation is difficult.

The object of the book is to provide an historical account of European and American tiles and to survey selected examples of their use in architecture. Tiles are not, of course, exclusive to Europe and America – Islamic tiles in the Middle East, or tiles in India and China, are examples of a rich heritage in other parts of the world, but it is beyond the scope of this book to include them.

What survives in Europe varies greatly from country to country. The reasons for the loss or survival of tiles are many, but probably nothing has been so destructive as the two World Wars. During the First World War, whole towns in Flanders and northern France were destroyed by shelling, while saturation bombing during the Second World War did immense damage to cities throughout Europe, particularly in Germany. There have also been calamities and natural disasters such as the Great Fire of London in 1666, or the earthquake that struck Lisbon in 1755.

Set of four tiles with stiff-leaf floral motifs from the Westminster Abbey Chapterhouse floor. Completed in 1259, and still *in situ*.

Changes in tastes and lifestyles have had equally far-reaching effects, leading to the replacement of old tiles by new, or by a different material altogether. The increasing use of wallpaper in the eighteenth and nineteenth centuries is a case in point. The restorers of buildings have also left their mark, particularly in the nineteenth century, when many medieval churches and cathedrals fell prey to architects such as Viollet-le-Duc in France or Sir George Gilbert Scott in Britain. This is one reason why much of our medieval tile heritage has been lost to nineteenth-century replacements. During the twentieth century the cause has sometimes been the fast pace of urban renewal. Holland was once famous for its tiled buildings and interiors, but is now a country with hardly any seventeenth-century tiles and relatively few eighteenth-century tiles *in situ*.

Luckily, the picture is not all bleak. Early examples have survived, most frequently in countries where the pace of industrialization, road-building and urban renewal has been slow. Certain parts of Italy, southern Spain and Portugal retain much of their original tile heritage, often in places of worship, in palaces, or in the houses of the aristocracy. Nineteenth- and early twentieth-century tiles can often be found in northern Europe and the United States, and an increased awareness of the wealth of the European and American tile heritage has come about, partly due to the interest of collectors, and partly due to the efforts of active conservation groups.

The phenomenon of the tile collector dates from the nineteenth century, and has had both a negative and a positive effect. Removing tiles from buildings divorces them from their original context and function; on the other hand, many tiles have thus been saved from destruction, and are now in public and private collections where the tile historian can study and categorize them. Unfortunately the demand for old tiles generated by collectors has also sometimes contributed to their loss *in situ*, particularly in Holland, Germany and England.

It is only fairly recently that conservation groups have begun lobbying for the retention and conservation of tiles *in situ*, often as part of a bid to preserve an entire building. Tiles add an element of extra quality to a building, and their preservation and repair is an urgent matter. It is hoped that the examples shown in this book will help to reinforce this plea, as well as recording instances of tiles in their original settings, which in some cases already no longer survive. If a building is lost, a photograph can be the only record for posterity.

There is still much to be studied. Decorative floor tiles from the Middle Ages are represented at various sites in Britain, while in southern Spain the medieval Moorish Alhambra Palace and its tile

Panel of glazed relief Gothic Revival tiles, with stylized flowers set within pointed arches and matching border tiles at top and bottom. Originally used to line the apse of Christ Church, Scarborough, they were made by the Campbell Brick & Tile Company of Stoke-on-Trent in 1876.

mosaics can still be admired today. The technique of polychrome painting on tin-glazed tiles spread northwards from Italy to the rest of Europe at the beginning of the sixteenth century, and culminated in the magnificent painted tiles and panels of the sixteenth, seventeenth and early eighteenth centuries, made by potters in Spain, Portugal and Holland. The Renaissance is one of the richest episodes in European tile production, when whole interior walls were clad from top to bottom with painted tiles. An echo of this development, often under the influence of the Dutch tile industry, occurred in France, Britain, Germany and Denmark.

During the Industrial Revolution, the major centres of tile production shifted once again to northern Europe, and significant changes in manufacturing techniques were introduced. Transfer printing on ceramic tiles was one of the most important, and was first practised in Liverpool during the second half of the eighteenth century. During the nineteenth century, Britain led the world in the mechanized production and decoration of tiles, and mass production during the second half of the nineteenth century made tiles both more cheaply and much more widely available than had previously been the case. Tiles were used in almost every church, public building and private home in Britain, and for a great variety of different purposes. These developments had a marked effect on tile production in the rest of Europe, even in America, where large-scale production began to cater for the demands of the New World. Individual designers and architects also influenced this growing industry; for example the designers Walter Crane, William Morris and William De Morgan in Britain, and the Spanish and Dutch architects Antonio Gaudí and Hendrikus Berlage.

In the present century, the Modernists' obsession with raw, unadorned concrete, glass and steel, pushed out most forms of architectural decoration, including tiles. The architectural transformation of many cities during the 1960s and 1970s saw the destruction of large numbers of nineteenth-century buildings, together with the loss of their tiling. Fortunately, with the creation of conservation areas and a renewed interest in decorative tiling from many Post-Modernist architects, this trend has slackened. Apart from the major tile manufacturers, there is now also an increasing number of craftsmen and women who have set up small tile workshops, and who produce hand-decorated tiles of astonishing variety. The account that follows and the examples shown will, hopefully, not only contribute to the preservation of the great wealth of historical tiles that are still extant, but also promote interest in the creative work being done by contemporary firms and tile artists.

1

FOR GOD AND EARTHLY PRINCES

Mosaic tiles set around a central, circular, inlaid tile depicting Richard I in combat. Dating from *circa* 1260 to 1280, these tiles were originally made for Chertsey Abbey, Surrey, and are now in the British Museum.

In the history of medieval tiles, two quite distinct traditions can be identified: one in northern Europe, and the other in Moorish Spain. The northern European tradition of tile-making coincided with the development of Gothic architecture, which flourished from the late twelfth to the early sixteenth century. During this period, tiles were used mainly for flooring in churches, castles and palaces, as only the clergy, kings and the aristocracy could afford such a luxury. In churches, the use of tiles was part of a general tendency to make churches more resplendent, while secular rulers used them to make their residences more comfortable, and as symbols of their earthly power and wealth.

Early fourteenth-century inlaid tile from the abbey of Saint-Bertin in Saint-Omer.

MEDIEVAL TILES IN NORTHERN EUROPE

After the fall of the Roman Empire, during the Dark Ages, most buildings were constructed of wood. It was not until the tenth century, when the economy of western Europe revived, that more stone buildings, particularly churches, began to be built. If floors in wooden buildings had often been made of beaten earth, stone buildings required something more durable. Before ceramic floor tiles became widely used, however, other materials were employed, such as mosaic, marble and stone.

Mosaic floors were a legacy from Roman building traditions, where floors had been constructed out of small cubes of stone or marble. These tesserae were fitted closely together and embedded in cement to form geometric or figurative designs. Such *opus tessellatum* floors persisted until the early Middle Ages, particularly where Roman decorative traditions had been kept alive, as in many parts of southern Europe. The tenth-century Romanesque church of Sant Pau del Camp, Carrer de Sant Pau, in Barcelona still has part of its original black and white mosaic floor in place.

A special kind of decorative technique, known as 'Cosmati' work, developed in Italy during the twelfth and thirteenth centuries. It was made by cutting different kinds of coloured marble into flat shapes of various sizes, and was used to create elaborate inlaid floors. It was also applied to walls and church furnishings such as tombs and thrones. 'Cosmati' comes from the inscribed names of the Cosmas family, left on several such works carried out by them, for example in the Duomo at Anagni in 1231. It is very striking, but limited to surface decoration.

Cosmati workers served not only Italian patrons, but also took on commissions from abroad. A splendid Cosmati pavement (still *in situ*) was made for the area in front of the High Altar of Westminster Abbey from 1259 to 1268, under the patronage of Henry III. It is approximately seven metres square, and follows an intricate geometric design of roundels and rectangular panels.

Stone tiles were used to make another type of decorative floor. In Pas-de-Calais in northern France, a kind of white limestone was found which, when polished, looked not unlike alabaster. Square tiles were cut from this stone, and then decorated with inlaid designs. The stone was first polished, and the designs cut or engraved into it. The depressions were then filled with brown, red, grey or black mastic. However, this infill quickly wore away, and was not long-lasting. It survived better when it was employed for the decoration of gravestones, which were less frequently walked upon. Some very good thirteenth-century slabs of this kind have survived in the Cathédral de Notre-Dame, Saint-Omer, particularly in the lesser-used side chapels, and show elaborate geometric and figurative designs. These inlaid stone pavers are sometimes seen as the precursors of medieval ceramic inlaid tiles.

The earliest surviving medieval ceramic floor tiles have been excavated from sites in England, at York, Peterborough, St Albans and Winchester. These Saxon tiles of the late tenth or early eleventh century have geometric relief decorations in the form of raised lines, covered with lead glaze. They have been keyed on the back with small stab marks, to help their adhesion to the mortar. Some have flanges on their backs, which could indicate that they were used on the risers of steps or perhaps on a wall. These tiles, which certainly predate the Norman Conquest of 1066, are an isolated phenomenon and

OPPOSITE
Cosmati pavement in front of the High Altar at Westminster Abbey. It was commissioned by the Abbot of Westminster when he visited Rome in 1259, and laid in 1268.

appear to have been made only for the wealth-iest Anglo-Saxon minsters. No sustained tradi-tion developed from them, but they indicate the early use and significance of tiles.

It is now generally recognized that the main developments in early ceramic tile production took place in France towards the end of the twelfth century, and probably spread from there to Britain via Normandy. By the middle of the thirteenth century the ceramic tile industry was firmly established, not only in France and Britain, but also in the Low Countries and Ger-many. One reason for its widespread adoption could have been economic. Marble was ex-pensive and had to be imported, whereas clay was usually locally available and could be worked quickly and easily. The numerous abbeys then being built in northern Europe often had their churches and chapterhouses floored with ceramic tiles, while apartments in some contemporary royal residences, for example Westminster Palace, were also tiled.

A second reason can be found in the clear link between the use of decorative floor tiles and the beginnings of Gothic architecture. In the Romanesque period, buildings had been quite austere, but Gothic architecture began to show more colour and decoration, and orna-mental ceramic floor tiles were part of that development.

In medieval tile production, three main types can be distinguished: mosaic tiles, inlaid tiles and relief tiles. The production of medieval mosaic tiles for floors should not be confused with Roman mosaic. The latter was composed of small stone cubes, while medieval mosaic was made from pieces of red-fired clay of various shapes, which were assembled to form geometric patterns. Colour contrast was achieved by coating the pieces with slip – that

is, clay that has been diluted to a liquid con-sistency with water – and lead glazes, and in alternating dark-coloured tiles with light. Tile makers at that time could produce five different colour effects – brown by applying the trans-parent lead glaze directly to the red tile body, yellow by coating the tile first with white slip and then with a lead glaze, green by adding copper to the lead glaze (which was then again applied to pieces covered with white slip), dark green by applying the same copper/lead glaze directly to the red tile body, and a near black by applying a copper-saturated lead glaze to it.

Tile shapes were cut out of processed clay with the aid of wooden templates, and allowed to dry leather hard. An allowance was made for about ten per cent shrinkage during the drying and firing stages, and the tiles were cut at a slight angle, so that the surfaces of the sides tapered inwards. When the tiles were laid, the top surfaces would touch, but the tapered sides allowed the mortar to squeeze in between the tiles for firmer adhesion to the floor. The

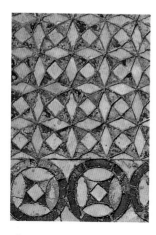

The ruins of the Cistercian monastery of Byland Abbey, near the village of Coxwold in North Yorkshire, contain some of the best-preserved thirteenth-century mosaic floor tiles in Europe. The most extensive areas survive in what used to be the presbytery and south transept. The tiles that were used as the risers for steps in front of the High Altar, and thus never walked upon, retain most of their original yellow and green glazed surface, and can give some idea of the original splendour of the floors.

ABOVE
Fine examples of different mosaic tile patterns and motifs from Byland Abbey.

RIGHT
Byland Abbey, North Yorkshire. One of the large surviving areas of medieval mosaic floor tiles.

medieval practice was to add the lead glaze to the as-yet unfired pieces, and to burn the 'green', unfired clay and glaze together in one firing. This had advantages and disadvantages. Applying the glaze directly to the unfired or 'green' tile saved fuel, time, labour and cost, and glaze applied to an unfired tile usually bonds better with it. However, during the firing, the presence of the glaze might itself prevent oxygen reaching the inner core of the tile, and could result in grey patches appearing on the red body, indicative of tiles which have not been properly fired.

It must be remembered that medieval kilns were rather primitive. Brick kilns were constructed and fired with brushwood, but they had none of the devices for measuring temperature that are now available. Success depended on the experience of the craftsmen involved. That is perhaps one reason why medieval tiles can vary so greatly. No two batches of tiles

turned out exactly alike, and to the modern eye, the diversity of their appearance is an attractive visual element.

The making of a good mosaic floor required considerable skill and experience, particularly in those instances where large circular pavements, often resembling a Gothic rose window, were part of the design. A circular pavement necessarily means that the pieces converge toward the centre, so each individual piece had to be cut to an exact size to fit an exact position in the overall design. This could be one reason why these complicated mosaic designs were abandoned toward the middle of the thirteenth century, in favour of square tiles laid out in square patterns.

We know little about the craftsmen who made the great early mosaic floors in Britain and France. It is probable that they travelled from site to site as buildings neared completion, since tiled floors were always laid towards the end of building operations. The tiles would usually have been made on site, as fixed production centres would have meant transporting them over long distances, which would have been impossible at that time unless navigable waterways were to hand. It is also possible that some of the early mosaic pavements in Britain were laid by travelling French craftsmen, before native potters took over. None of the early medieval tilers have emerged by name, and their anonymity is indicative of the medieval attitude towards the arts, whereby the end-product mattered far more than the individual who had made it.

Different mosaic shapes, and a few contrasting colours, resulted in a remarkable range of different patterns. These were usually geometric, but simple figurative shapes such as fleurs-de-lis, stylized leaves and birds could also be

Thirteenth-century mosaic tiles near the site of the High Altar in the sanctuary at Fountains Abbey, North Yorkshire. A range of complex patterns has been made out of simple geometrical shapes, carefully cut and fitted closely together.

incorporated. Floors were laid out in bands, with different zones containing varying combinations of mosaic patterns. Examples of such early mosaic floors include, in France, Notre-Dame-du-Parc at Rouen, and the Abbaye de la Sauve Majeure near Bordeaux, both of the late twelfth or early thirteenth century. In Britain, towards the middle of the thirteenth century, some splendid mosaic floors were laid in various Cistercian abbeys, among which Fountains, Byland, Rievaulx and Meaux Abbey, all in Yorkshire, are fine examples. At Byland large areas of tile mosaic can still be seen in their original location.

Uncertainty surrounds a definite place of origin for the two-colour inlaid tile, but it first appeared during the second quarter of the thirteenth century. Its distinctive characteristic is that a pattern or design is inlaid into the red body of the tile. The main method of manufacture was to use a wooden stamp to imprint a design in sunken relief into the surface of the tile while it was still green. This was then filled with white clay and left to dry. Once leather hard, surplus white clay was scraped off to reveal the white, inlaid design against the red body of the tile. The tile was then covered with a transparent lead glaze and fired. The lead glaze made the red body of the tile appear brown, and turned the white inlaid clay yellow. Other techniques for inlaying the white clay were also developed, one of which was the 'stamp on slip' method. The tile would be covered with white slip, and once leather hard, a wooden stamp was used to force this into the red tile body, with the surplus again being scraped away.

The French architectural
historian and restorer
Viollet-le-Duc frequently
removed badly worn
medieval fittings such as
tiles from the buildings he
worked on, and replaced
them with nineteenth-
century copies. However,
he was careful to study
and record details of the
original material before it
was removed. During his
restoration of the chapels
at the east end of Saint-
Denis in Paris in the early
1850s, he measured and
drew the medieval floors
in the various apsidal
chapels, on the basis of
which replica tiles were
made and laid down
under his supervision.

LEFT
Tile mosaic of interlacing
squares and circles in the
Chapelle de la Vierge,
Saint-Denis, Paris. The
tiles are faithful
nineteenth-century copies
of the late twelfth-century
originals.

RIGHT
Mosaic tiles in the
Chapelle de Saint
Cucuphas, Saint-Denis,
Paris. Mosaic patterns such
as circles and quatrefoils
are inlaid into larger tiles,
creating two-colour effects
which herald the later
two-colour inlaid tile.
Again, these tiles are exact
copies of the twelfth-
century originals.

OPPOSITE
The Westminster Abbey
Chapterhouse, London,
completed in 1259, still
retains its medieval floor.
It is in a remarkably good
state of preservation and
shows a wealth of
patterns, devices and
figurative scenes, laid in
parallel bands of square
tiles, separated by strips of
rectangular tiles. Motifs
include, as shown here,
the royal coat of arms of
Henry III, a clear
indication that the tiles
were made under his
patronage.

However the result was achieved, it allowed for greater decorative possibilities and an increased range of subject matter. Early patterns were usually quite simple – for example six-petal rosettes, running borders and fleurs-de-lis designs. The fleurs-de-lis motif in particular was popular, as it was both the royal insignia of France, and the emblem of the Virgin Mary. The early thirteenth-century inlaid tiles at the Abbaye de Saint-Pierre-sur-Dives in Normandy display, apart from stylized floral designs, geometric patterns and decorative borders, some figurative designs containing birds, lions and deer. The symbolism of these animals was significant. The lion, for example, symbolized power, courage, virtue and the Resurrection.

Medieval French figurative tiles were more than matched in Britain by the great surviving pavement in Westminster Abbey Chapterhouse, which, like that in front of the High Altar, was also laid under the patronage of Henry III, and was completed in 1259. Here we

find a most imposing range of tiles, depicting heraldic lions and the royal coat of arms, as well as figurative scenes on single tiles of a bishop, a king and queen, musicians and hunting scenes. The most famous tile shows King Edward the Confessor giving a ring to St John the Baptist, who has appeared before him in the guise of a pilgrim. Tiles began to be used to contribute to the overall iconographic programme of churches and chapterhouses, along with stained glass, stone carvings and painted ceilings.

Perhaps the most famous surviving thirteenth-century tiles (although unfortunately not in their original location) are the inlaid tiles from Chertsey Abbey in Surrey, which were probably made between 1250 and 1290. The best among them are high-quality inlaid roundels, depicting the romance of Tristram and Iseult, and a further set known as the 'Richard the Lion-Heart series'. These demonstrate the complex subjects that could be illustrated using the inlaid technique, and were seldom equalled

RIGHT
A late thirteenth-century
lead-glazed inlaid tile from
Thornton Abbey, South
Humberside. It shows a
daisy within a circle, and
has petal-shaped corner
motifs.

FAR RIGHT
Four late fifteenth-century
lead-glazed inlaid tiles,
each bearing the
inscription *AVE MARIA*,
from the demolished
church of Meaux Abbey,
Yorkshire. The heart-
shaped petal motif forms a
central flower.

Section of circular pavement from the King's Chapel, Clarendon Palace, near Salisbury, dated 1240−44 (now in the British Museum). It demonstrates the high level of technical skill achieved by the medieval tiler in creating complex mosaic pavements from inlaid tiles of different shapes. The inscription at the top reads *PAVIMENTUM HENRICI REGIS ANGLIE* ('The pavement of Henry the King of the English').

During the Middle Ages, fireplace bricks were essential to shield wooden houses from the risk of fire. Later, in stone-built dwellings, fireplace bricks continued to be used to fireproof the back of fireplaces, and were often decorated with moulded patterns or figurative motifs. The brick illustrated here is probably of a sixteenth-century date, and was made in the Low Countries. It depicts Adam and Eve.

Sixteenth-century Dutch lead-glazed inlaid floor tile. The inscription in Gothic letters around the central diamond reads *ALLE DINC HEEFT SIJNEN TIJT* ('For everything there is a season'). The heraldic shield bears the emblem of the Dukes of Burgundy.

after the thirteenth century.

Inlaid tiles were not restricted to ecclesiastical buildings; as has been said, royal palaces were also paved with them. Clarendon Palace near Salisbury had inlaid tiles which were laid towards the middle of the thirteenth century, and several rooms at Westminster Palace were paved between 1238 and 1250. In France, Château de Suscinio, at Morbihan near Vannes in south-west Brittany, was paved with two-colour tiles.

In the fourteenth century, the expanding market for inlaid tiles resulted in several changes in production. The shape of the tile now mattered less, since designs often extended over more than one, with individual elements linking up to create larger overall patterns. This differed from tile mosaic, where the shape of the tile was as significant as its colour. Since square and rectangular shapes could be cut more easily and quickly than complicated mosaic tiles, most fourteenth-century and later tiles are square. Whereas abbeys and royal palaces had previously been the tilers' principal customers, tiles were now also bought for parish churches, and sometimes even for the town houses of the well-to-do. Tile factories were established in areas where there was a sufficient demand, and could supply customers within a given distance.

In Holland during the fourteenth century, various ceramic workshops supplying tiles, bricks, roof tiles and everyday wares were often established just outside the town walls, because of the fire risk from the kilns to adjacent wooden buildings. There they became part of the urban economy. Utrecht in central Holland provides a good example of this. During the Middle Ages Utrecht was a large and prosperous town. The use of roof tiles, bricks and floor tiles was promoted by the municipal authorities as a fire prevention measure, and subsidies were given to encourage this. Tiles were therefore found not only in Utrecht's various churches, but were also installed in the houses of wealthy clergy. A very fine floor, probably dating from the first half of the fourteenth century and containing plain, inlaid and even a few tin-glazed tiles, was uncovered in 1862 on the site of the house of a former canon of Sint Janskerk in Utrecht.

Two unglazed fourteenth-century German line-impressed tiles, with a stiff-leaf foliage design. German floor tiles were not glazed, and relied for effect on the tiles having clay bodies of contrasting colours. The tiles shown here came from the chapel of Schloss Schönburg, Oberwesel-am-Rhein.

Unglazed fourteenth-century German line-impressed tile, with a design of a heraldic eagle.

The less well-off were nonetheless able to afford plain glazed tiles for the most important rooms in their houses. The shift away from exclusively ecclesiastical and royal to secular use is also evident in Britain, where square, fourteenth-century inlaid tiles have been found at Clifton House, King's Lynn, in Norfolk, and a late fifteenth- or early sixteenth-century floor (now in the British Museum) was discovered at Canynges House in Bristol. In France, glazed geometric, encaustic and relief tiles were also applied to the facades of houses during the late fifteenth and early sixteenth centuries, particularly in the Pré d'Auge, Champagne and Beauvais regions. La Maison aux Faience in Beauvais was a well-known example, until it was destroyed by fire in June 1940. Patronage expanded along with wealth and power, from the church and the aristocracy to the merchants, with wealthy merchants apparently adopting the same tiling schemes that were once limited to religious and royal establishments.

The third type of medieval tile, which developed separately from mosaic and inlaid tiles, was the relief tile. This can be decorated either with raised relief or sunken counter-relief. The technique may have originated in Germany and spread to Britain via the Low Countries, as relief tiles are common in Germany east of the Rhine, where they were made from the latter half of the twelfth century onwards. They were usually unglazed, with variety being achieved by using grey and red firing clays, and alternating the tiles on the floor. The designs on many German relief tiles can often be better described as 'line impressed', since they consist only of a simple outline impressed in the clay, describing mainly stylized Gothic foliage, geometric patterns or sometimes heraldic lions. Such tiles, dating from the thirteenth and fourteenth reconquest was slow and piecemeal. Cordoba was recaptured in 1236 and Seville in 1248. The roles were now reversed, and Moors lived under Christian rule. Moorish artists and craftsmen served Christian patrons and a strange mixture of Christian and Moorish culture resulted. In architecture and design this is known as the '*Mudejar*' style, and it continued until the fifteenth century. Granada, ruled by the Nasrids, was not reconquered until 1492. It was here that the most extraordinary flowering of late Moorish art and architecture took place, resulting in the construction of one of the most celebrated buildings in the world, the Alhambra Palace.

Moorish tile mosaic differs greatly from the medieval mosaic tiles used in northern Europe. Firstly, it was mainly used on walls. This follows a well-established tradition in the Middle East, where the walls of mosques and palaces were often completely covered with tile mosaic or painted tiles. The colour range of the mosaic tiles in southern Spain is extensive, with blue, orange, green, violet, brown, black and white predominating. Moreover, unlike northern European mosaic tiles, where each piece was cut from unfired clay, the Moors cut their tiles from slabs that had already been fired and glazed. This technique, which allowed for closer and more exact fitting, first appeared in Spain in the thirteenth century. Moorish tile mosaic relies on its varied shapes and colour contrasts for visual interest, and never incorporates figurative elements. This is very different from northern medieval practice, where tiles were inlaid with various figurative motifs from the middle of the thirteenth century onwards. Islamic Hadith literature, in which the traditions associated with the Prophet Mohammed's life are recorded, states in one passage concerning the question of who are the enemies of God, that 'the maker of images of pictures is the enemy of God', therefore much Islamic art shuns figurative representations.

Moorish tile mosaic can still be found on and in several buildings in southern Spain. The Torre del Oro, on the banks of the Rio Guadalquivir in Seville, was built in the early thirteenth century by the ruling Almohads, as a defensive structure for their castle, the Alcázar. Some mosaic has survived at the very top of the tower, above the window openings in the wall. Once Seville had reverted to Christian rule, tile mosaic made by Moorish craftsmen continued to be used for churches and palaces. The church of Omnium Sanctorum has fourteenth-century tile mosaic above the central window over the entrance door, while in the sanctuary of San Gil the walls are covered with different types of tile mosaic. The most spectacular example of mosaic work in Seville is in the Palace of Peter the Cruel in the Alcázar, built for him by Moorish craftsmen or *mudejares*. The palace has a central court known as the Patio de Las Doncellas (Court of the Maidens), which has fine Moorish arches and walls covered with various forms of tile mosaic. Rooms leading off from the courtyard have extensive mosaic tiling, contrasting with elaborately worked plaster decorations. Much of this tiling was renovated in the fifteenth century under the rule of Ferdinand and Isabella.

Beyond question, the most outstanding example of tile mosaic in Spain is the Alhambra Palace in Granada. The Alhambra was built for the ruling Nasrid family in the fourteenth century, and from the outside appears rather plain. It is the interiors of the various courtyards and the rooms leading off them that display all the refined splendour of Moorish

Complex white linear arabesque patterns, characteristic of fifteenth-century *Mudejar* tile mosaic, in the courtyard of the Palace of Peter the Cruel.

The fourteenth-century Palace of Peter the Cruel is the
heart of the Alcázar in Seville. It consists of a central
courtyard surrounded by various rooms with ornate
Mudejar tile and plaster work. The courtyard has striking
lobe-shaped arches supported by slender columns, while
the walls are richly decorated with tile mosaic. It is
characterized by the use of thin white glazed strips between
the sections of coloured tiles, resulting in complex patterns
of white interlacing bands. The Salon of the Ambassadors
and the Bedroom of the Moorish Kings lead off from the
courtyard and are connected via a maze of smaller rooms.
Striking tile patterns and rich stucco decoration are
prominent features of them all.

ABOVE
Tiled dado in the courtyard of the Palace of Peter the Cruel.

RIGHT
Detail of the tile mosaic in the courtyard of the Palace of
Peter the Cruel.

A tiled column in the
Mexuar Court of the
Alhambra Palace.

The refined Moorish culture of the Nasrid rulers of Granada reached its peak under Yusuf I (1333–53), and Muhammed V (1353–91), with the building of the Alhambra Palace. The Alhambra is one of the most visually stunning buildings in Islamic architecture: an intricate succession of chambers and courtyards, decorated with slender columns, water basins and fountains. The stone walls of the palace are covered with tile mosaic and ornate plasterwork, and the contrast between the ornate linear patterns and calligraphic inscriptions on the plaster, and the rich colours of the geometric tiles is wholly successful. The infinite patterns and arabesque designs seem to dematerialize the walls, and thus express a basic characteristic of Islamic art – the dissolution of matter.

ABOVE
Detail of the wall mosaic in the Court of the Myrtle Trees.

BELOW
Detail of the wall mosaic in the Hall of the Ambassadors.

OPPOSITE
The Court of the Myrtle Trees in the Alhambra.

A fifteenth-century tin-glazed *socarrat* tile from Valencia, bearing the emblem of Castile and León, painted in blue. The boldness and clarity of the design is typical of this type of tile.

Mudejar-style window above the entrance of the fourteenth-century church of Omnium Sanctorum, Seville. The window has a double scalloped arch, with a larger horseshoe arch superimposed. The areas between the two are filled with tile mosaic.

Detail of the *Mudejar* dome in the Convento de la Concepcion, Toledo. Fragments of early fifteenth-century blue-and-white and yellow lustre tiles decorate the ceiling of the dome.

architecture and decoration. Delicately carved Moorish archways on slender columns combine with exquisite plaster work and colourful mosaic tiles, together with fountains and pools of water. The main tiled areas in the Alhambra are the Mexuar, the Mexuar Court and the Court of the Myrtle Trees, off which are the Barca Gallery, the Hall of the Ambassadors and the fabulous Court of the Lions, which used to be the heart of the harem section of the palace. From here access is gained to the Hall of the Two Sisters, the Kings' Chamber and the Abencerrajes Gallery. The spectacular tiling is mainly in the form of a dado running along the lower parts of the walls, with ornate plaster work immediately above.

Two rooms stand out: the Hall of the Ambassadors and the Hall of the Two Sisters. The first, which used to be the audience chamber of the Moorish kings, has varied tile mosaic work all round the room. It also has a remarkable ornate cedarwood ceiling, and large tiled window openings. These run down to the level of the floor, with magnificent views of the massive snowcapped mountains of the Sierra Nevada. On the floor of this room there are still some blue-and-white painted lustre tiles with the Nasrid motto 'There is no Conqueror but God'. The Hall of the Two Sisters was described by the American essayist Washington Irving in his famous set of romantic stories, *Tales of the Alhambra*, first published in 1832. Acute observation is mixed with romance when he writes:

On one side of the court a portal, richly adorned, opens into a lofty hall paved with white marble and called the Hall of the Two Sisters. A *cúpola* or lantern admits a tempered light from above and a free circulation of air. The lower part of the walls is encrusted with beautiful Moorish tiles, on some of which are emblazoned the escutcheons of the Moorish monarchs; the upper part is faced with the fine stucco-work invented in Damascus, . . . On each side of the hall are recesses for ottomans and couches. Above an inner porch is a balcony which communicated with the women's apartment. The latticed *jalousies* still remain, from whence the dark-eyed beauties of the harem might gaze unseen upon the entertainment in the hall below.

Although most of the tile work at the Alhambra is in the form of mosaic, some painted tiles were also used. However, few of these have remained in their original position. Many were carried off by nineteenth-century collectors, although some good specimens found during excavations are preserved in the Museo de Arte Hispano-Musulman (Palacio de Carlos V) at the Alhambra. These tiles are tin glazed with decorations painted in blue, and occasionally have details picked out in overglaze lustre. This type of tile became a much sought-after product of the Moorish craftsmen, not only in Málaga and Granada but also in Valencia.

Despite the fact that Valencia had permanently reverted to Christian rule by 1238, Moorish craftsmen remained and worked in the region, and tin-glazed pottery had been produced in and around Valencia since the twelfth century. The technique was first developed in the Middle East, and reached Spain with the Moorish occupation. Early wares were usually painted in green and a purple-brown, but blue and lustre decoration was introduced in the fourteenth century, probably under the influence of Moorish potters from Andalusia in southern Spain. A great deal of pottery was made in just two suburbs of Valencia, Manises and Paterna, which became famous throughout Europe for their blue-and-white and lustre pottery and tiles. In contrast to the Islamic tradition, Valencian fifteenth-century blue-and-white tin-glazed tiles show a remarkable range of figurative subject matter, including animals, the human figure, faces, heraldic motifs, abstract patterns and Christian religious symbols. A very different kind of tile was the so-called '*socarrat*' or ceiling tile. These were large square or rectangular tiles, placed between the ceiling beams. They were painted in dark blue, red or black, often directly onto the unglazed surface of the tile, with bold, stylized designs that make them very pleasing to the modern eye. These include patterned motifs, animals and men on horseback, depicted with great clarity and a sure touch of the brush.

Valencian tin-glazed pottery with blue and gold or copper lustre designs was exported across Europe, where it often took pride of place among the possessions of those who could afford it. Valencian tiles were also in demand. Tin-glazed tiles with the old-fashioned green and purple-brown colour scheme were used as floor tiles in the Papal Palace at Avignon in 1362, while the Dukes of Burgundy had a particular liking for blue-and-white tiles embellished with lustre. Records have survived of these tiles being made for ducal residences and religious houses under ducal protection. Jean, Duc de Berry had lustre tile pavements made with his coats of arms for the Palais de Justice in Poitiers between 1384 and 1386, but instead of having the tiles made at Valencia, a Moorish tile maker referred to in

the accounts as 'le Sarrazin' went to Poitiers to carry out the commission. Only a few surviving tiles have been excavated.

The pictorial record of Spanish blue-and-white tiles in fifteenth-century Flemish paintings by Jan van Eyck, and in others ascribed to Petrus Christus, is also of interest, and may provide some information as to how these tiles were actually arranged on the floor. In some of these pictures they are represented with such accuracy that their actual designs can be identified. Van Eyck's *Madonna with Canon George van der Paele* of 1434–6, now in the Groeningemuseum, Bruges, has blue-and-white Valencian-type tiles with Moorish interlacing patterns arranged as groups of four, set among plain, late medieval, brown lead-glazed tiles. *The Fountain of Life* in the Prado, ascribed to Petrus Christus, is particularly interesting, as it shows blue-and-white tin-glazed tiles used to pave an area immediately below a heavenly company, while the men and women at the bottom of the picture stand on plain lead-glazed tiles. It could be argued from this that the highly valued Valencian blue-and-white tiles were rare and precious enough, in fifteenth-century northern Europe, to be used to identify and enhance the holy spaces shown in paintings.

Italy's proximity to and trading links with the Middle East meant that the tin-glaze technique found its way there from an early date, but the main developments in pottery and tile manufacture in Italy did not take place until the fifteenth century, when it grew into a flourishing industry during the Renaissance. It is from this basis that the next great phase in the history of tiles in European architecture springs.

2

PAINTED MAGNIFICENCE

The eighteenth-century gardens of the Palácio do Visconde de Estoi, in the Algarve, Portugal, are built up in balustraded terraces, which lead to the palace. The terraces themselves are decorated with statues, set within tiled niches.

The great developments in art in fifteenth-century Italy included the production of painted maiolica floor tiles. Although the origins of tin-glazed tiles are to be found in Spain, Italy became the first important European centre of production for painted tiles. At the beginning of the sixteenth century, émigré potters from northern Italy introduced the maiolica technique to Spain, France and Flanders, from where it spread to Holland and Portugal. These two countries became prominent producers in the seventeenth century. The Dutch eventually came to dominate the industry, with a lucrative tile export market throughout Europe. Smaller production centres were active during the eighteenth century in Britain,

English delftware tile, probably from Bristol, 1725–50. One of a group of six, illustrated on page 85.

Germany and Denmark, often initially with the help of Dutch potters. Painting with colour on white tin glaze can produce visual effects of startling vividness, and these were used to create tiling schemes of opulent splendour in palaces, churches and houses throughout Europe. Tiles again served as an index to status, and made magnificent the most prestigious architecture of Europe's flourishing nation-states, while the process of painting on tin glaze responded to the inventive spirit of the Renaissance.

ITALY

Much of what we know of fifteenth- and early sixteenth-century Italian tin-glazed pottery techniques comes from a treatise of 1557 entitled the *Three Books of the Potter's Art*, by an Italian potter called Piccolpasso. It covers such matters as the preparation of the clay, the forming of vases, various pottery tools and kilns, and the composition of glazes, ceramic pigments and lustres. However, tin-glazed pottery had been made in Italy since the twelfth century. By the thirteenth century much green and purple-brown ware was being produced at Orvieto. The earliest examples of maiolica, as Italian painted tin-glazed pottery is known, are therefore also referred to as 'Orvieto ware'. During the first half of the fifteenth century, under the influence of Valencian pottery, Italian potters began to use blue decoration on a white ground, sometimes with the addition of purple. Orange, blue and yellow were introduced later in the century, enabling spectacular colour combinations to be created. Added to this was the lustre technique, also transmitted from Spain.

Tin glaze is lead glaze to which tin-oxide has been added, which has the effect of turning the

Two mid-fifteenth-century hexagonal maiolica floor tiles, depicting the head of a woman in profile, and two pomegranates. Both tiles are very finely painted.

glaze an opaque white. The method of production itself is fairly time-consuming and complicated. The tiles were first cut to the required shape from suitable clay, and then fired at about 1000°C. This first firing is known as the 'biscuit' firing. After this the tin glaze would be applied, and when it was dry, the painter transferred a design onto the unfired white glaze by pricking it through a piece of paper. Charcoal was dusted across the paper leaving the dotted outline of the design on the tile as a guide.

The pigments used by the tile painter were made from metal oxides: blue from cobalt, purple from manganese, green from copper, yellow from antimony, and orange from a combination of antimony and iron. The painter usually outlined the design first, and then filled in the required shades and colours. Painting on unfired tin glaze is like painting on blotting paper; mistakes cannot be corrected, so great sureness of touch is required. The tile was then fired again, causing the tin glaze to turn into a glassy white coat. The colours sank into the glaze and fused permanently with it. The technique is therefore known as 'in-glaze' decoration. Sometimes a transparent glaze, known in Italian as '*coperta*', was added to enhance the brilliance of the tin glaze as well as the colours. Any additional lustre decoration would also require a further firing.

The tin-glaze technique in Europe came to be known under three principal names: 'maiolica', 'faience' and 'delft', all of which are themselves derived from the names of places involved in either trade or manufacture. 'Maiolica' derives from the island of Majorca, which was a major trading centre for tin-glazed ware during the fifteenth century. Maiolica pottery and tiles were manufactured in Deruta, Urbino, Gubbio and Castel Durante, among

Hexagonal maiolica floor tile, *circa* 1465, from the Duomo at Capua. It shows a craftsman at work.

Mid-eighteenth-century cruciform maiolica floor tile with an arabesque motif, made in Faenza. Similar tiles are still *in situ* in the chapel of Palazzo Ferniani in Faenza.

ISAB ESTE·MR MAN

Early sixteenth-century maiolica floor tiles, made for the private *studiolo* of Isabella d'Este at her palace in Mantua. The octagonal tile bears the inscription *ISAB[ELLA] ESTE[NIS] MAR[CHIONESSA] MAN[TUA]*.

other places. 'Faience' probably comes from the Italian town of Faenza, where much tin-glazed pottery was manufactured (most Italian centres of ceramic production were situated in the north of the country). 'Delftware' refers to the Dutch town of Delft, which became a major centre of production during the seventeenth and eighteenth centuries.

During the Renaissance, the main use of tiles was for floors. They were made in various shapes, usually square or hexagonal, but triangular, round and star-shaped tiles are also known. Some early Italian tiles, dated 1440–45, have survived from the Cappella Caracciolo del Sole in San Giovanni a Carbonara, Naples, arranged in what was then the conventional manner, featuring a square tile framed by four elongated hexagons, the five together forming a larger octagon. Many of these tiles, painted in blue with added touches of purple and green, display floral designs or geometrical patterns that show a Valencian influence. This is not surprising, as tiles made in Valencia were imported to Italy throughout the fifteenth century.

Italian painted floor tiles complemented other features of church interiors, such as marble altarpieces and frescoes on the walls. In this way a carefully integrated decorative scheme was achieved for the whole. In the Cappella Mazzatosta in Santa Maria della Verità, Viterbo, predominantly blue and purple tiles with bold foliate designs and profile heads form rich patterns that contrast with the more monumental frescoes by Lorenzo da Viterbo. The frescoes were finished in 1469 and the pavement laid shortly after.

Handsome tiles with a rich colour range of blue, orange and green were laid in the Cappella di San Sebastiano of the Vaselli family in

Square maiolica floor tile, made between 1503 and 1513, depicting the arms of Pope Julius II, the patron of Michelangelo. It is decorated with the triple crown, the crossed keys of St Peter and the Latin inscription *IVL II* (Julius II).

San Petronio, Bologna. A tile inscribed with the year 1487 gives us a firm date. Most of the tiles are hexagonal, with intricate and varied patterns carefully designed to fit that shape, together with tiles bearing figurative images such as animals and human heads in profile. They have been attributed to the workshop of Pietro de Andrea in Faenza.

Tiles with emblematic devices were also used for the floors of papal buildings. In Castel Sant'-Angelo, Rome, square tiles were used in rooms furnished during the reign of Pope Nicholas V (1447–55). Some of these tiles (now in the Museo di Castel Sant'Angelo) are painted in dark blue and bear the papal device of the triple crown and the two crossed keys of St Peter, while others have different emblems of the papacy executed in blue, purple and yellow.

The famous patron of the arts, Isabella d'Este, ordered tiles for her palace in Mantua in 1494. These were decorated with coats of arms and a variety of elaborate and colourful armorial

OPPOSITE
Late fifteenth- or early sixteenth-century maiolica pavement, attributed to the della Robbia workshop, in the Loggias of Raphael in the Vatican. The tile painter has copied a Hispano-Moresque design very closely. The taste for Spanish patterns may have come from the Borgia Pope Alexander VI (r. 1492–1503), who was of Spanish descent.

View of the eighteenth-century garden behind Santa Chiara in Naples. The tiles on the columns are painted with swirling flowers and foliage, while the benches have tile panels of landscapes. The tiles were made locally at the beginning of the 1740s.

devices with inscriptions in different languages. A tile depicting a white unicorn with the German motto *BIDER CRAFT* ('Righteous Strength') is especially notable, as is one with a gauntlet and the Spanish motto *BUENA FE NONES MUDABLE* ('True love never falters'). Octagonal tiles bearing Isabella d'Este's own name were made *circa* 1525 for her private *studiolo*.

By the end of the fifteenth century, Italian potters had established a strong tradition of painted images of great variety, executed in bright colours on single tiles. They had also absorbed technical influences from Spain. With the arrival of the Italian potter, Francisco Niculoso, in Seville at the beginning of the sixteenth century, it was the turn of the Italians to leave their mark on the development of Spanish tile painting.

SPAIN

The special character of Niculoso's painted tiles can only be fully appreciated when they are seen against the native tile production of Seville at this period. Seville enjoyed a unique position among European centres of tile production, as the place where many varied techniques and influences met and were exchanged. There was the established tradition of tile mosaic, evident in the fourteenth-century Palace of Peter the Cruel in the Alcázar and in several Sevillian churches. There was also the technique of *cuerda seca*, which had begun to be used for tiles during the fifteenth century, in an attempt to solve the problem of how to combine different colours on a single tile without the pigments running into each other. *Cuerda seca* or 'dry-cord' consisted of drawing the outlines of the design with a compound of grease and iron-oxide. The design was then filled with different coloured glazes, and during firing the greasy lines kept the different colours apart. A similar technique was known as *cuenca*. In this the design was pressed into the tile with a mould that left it outlined with raised edges. The tile was then biscuit fired, after which the hollows were filled with coloured glazes.

Cuenca tiles were used extensively, and important early sixteenth-century examples still remain in Seville, for example both outside and inside the pavilion of Charles V in the gardens of the Alcázar. At the Casa de Pilatos (so called because its layout was supposed to have been based on that of the house of Pontius Pilate in Jerusalem), thousands of *cuenca* tiles cover the walls of the inner courtyard, adjacent rooms and the giant staircase, while *cuerda seca* tiles were used on the walls of the chapel. But the technique of pictorial maiolica painting introduced by Francisco Niculoso was new, and soon attracted the support of important patrons in Seville.

Dated works and documents record Niculoso's activities in Seville from 1503 to 1529. His earliest surviving signed work can still be seen in his own parish church of Santa Ana in Triana, a suburb of Seville. It takes the form of a tiled tomb for one Inigo Lopez, set against one of the lower walls at the back of the church. The memorial depicts the full-length painted figure of Lopez, and immediately above his head is the inscription *NICULOSO FRANCISCO ITALIANO ME FECIT*. The date 1503 appears as part of the dedicatory inscription.

In 1504 Niculoso was commissioned to make two tiled altars for the private oratory at the Alcázar in Seville of Isabella the Catholic, wife of Ferdinand V and joint ruler of Castile and Aragon from 1479 to 1504. One of these

survives, and has a tiled altarpiece of the Visitation. The tiled altar-front below shows the Annunciation. Both scenes demonstrate Niculoso's knowledge of fifteenth-century Italian panel and fresco painting, in terms of composition as well as of pictorial space, and a system of perspective with a central vanishing point is used with great effect. Both panels have elaborate borders with many supporting figures and allegorical symbols, and Niculoso's signature appears immediately below the Virgin in the Visitation scene. The effect of the application of maiolica colours to such a monumental scheme is magnificent, expressing both Renaissance aesthetics and state power.

Niculoso was also patronized by the Catholic

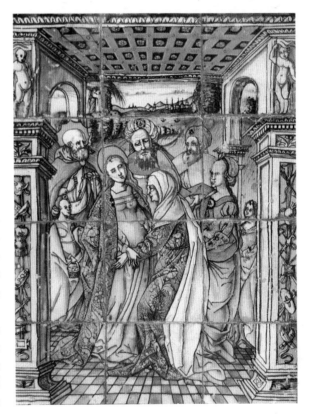

Early sixteenth-century tin-glazed panel, now in the Rijksmuseum, Amsterdam, depicting the Visitation. It is signed by Francisco Niculoso. A Renaissance interest in perspective can be seen in the use of the lines on the floor and ceiling to suggest a central vanishing point. The figures are thus placed within a convincing setting, and the illusion of a three-dimensional space is heightened by the view of a distant landscape.

Detail of a wall in the central courtyard of the Casa de Pilatos, showing a range of abstract *cuenca* tile motifs. The tiles in the panel at the bottom of the wall create the illusion of three-dimensional superimposed cubes, while the ornate plasterwork above them shows the Moorish influence of the Alhambra.

A *cuenca* tile at the Casa de Pilatos. The tiled coat of arms of León and Castile is surrounded and embellished with lustre.

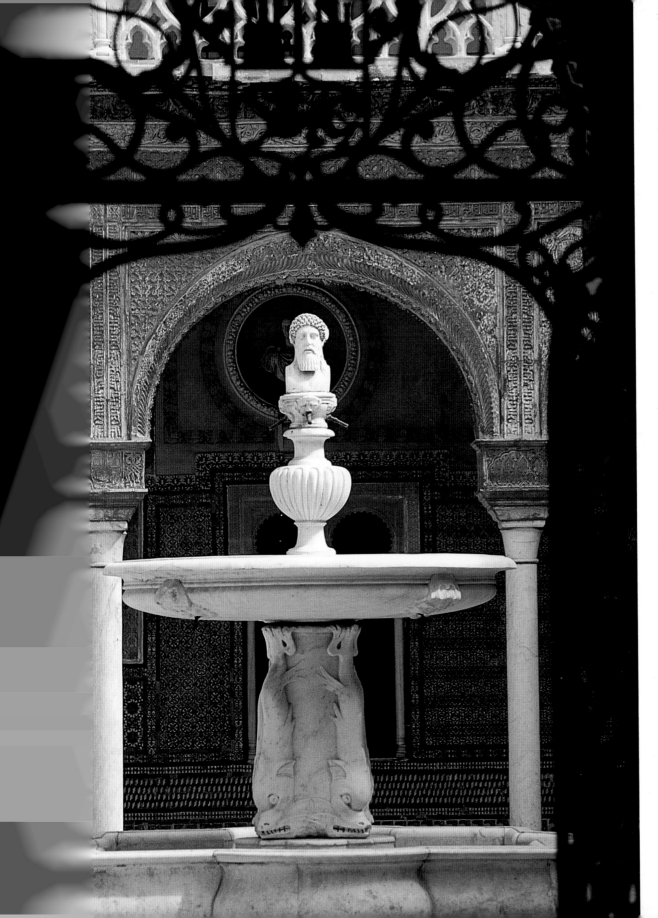

The Casa de Pilatos was built by the Marques de Tarifa in 1519, after he had undertaken a pilgrimage to the Holy Land. The layout of the house is supposed to be based on that of Pontius Pilate in Jerusalem. It is the most magnificent domestic residence in Seville, with a large central courtyard containing several classical statues. Stylistically, it is a curious blend of Moorish, Gothic, Byzantine and Renaissance architecture. The walls of the courtyard, the grand staircase and all the rooms on the ground floor are covered in *cuenca* and *cuerda seca* tiles, some of which are decorated with gold lustre. These tiled walls create a spectacular display of form and colour, as well as providing a cool refuge indoors during the heat of summer.

LEFT
View across the main courtyard of the Casa de Pilatos in Seville. Behind the fountain, walls encrusted with early sixteenth-century *cuenca* tiles can be seen.

Church. In 1504 he carried out work for the convent church of Santa Paula in Seville, painting a panel of St Paula to be placed over the gateway entrance to the convent, and making tiles for the upper half of the external portal of the church. In this he collaborated with the sculptor Pedro Millán. The pointed arch has seven polychrome faience relief roundels, made by Pedro Millán in the style of della Robbia, which are set against a background of Niculoso's tiles. Commissions also came from other parts of Spain – for instance a tiled altar for the monastery of Santa María de Tentudía, in the Sierra Morena foothills above the town of Calera de Leon.

After Niculoso's death in 1529 there seems to have been a brief lull in the production of maiolica panels. Production of *cuenca* tiles, however, was maintained on a large scale. Documents reveal renewed activity of tile

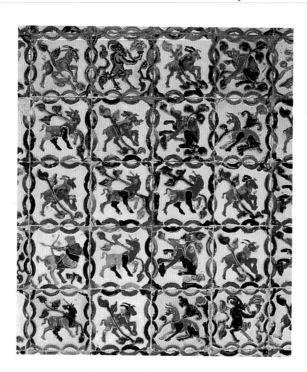

production in the *à lo romano* style from 1558 onwards. The arrival of Frans Andries, whose father Guido Andries was an Italian who had settled in Antwerp, introduced ideas of Antwerp-inspired mannerist design. It also illustrates how easily ideas of tile design and techniques made their way across Europe. Frans Andries entered into partnership with the Sevillian tile maker Roque Hernández in 1561, and many tiling schemes carried out during the second half of the sixteenth century attest to the influential role of what has come to be known as the Italo-Flemish style.

A major commission of this kind, which extended over several years, was the work done for the Salas de las Fiestas and Salas de las Bóvedas, now known as the Salón de Carlos V in the Alcázar. One of the principal tile makers involved was Christóbal de Augusta, son-in-law of Roque Hernández. These extensive rooms all have continuous high, tiled dados. Some sections of these are signed and dated 1577 and 1578. The walls are further divided into rectangular panels of various sizes, edged with borders at top and bottom. The influence of Italian mannerist design is clear in the grotesques, putti and complex strapwork, intermixed with fountains, sphinxes and candelabras. Yellow dominates as a background colour, followed by blue, orange, green and white. This kind of tiling was also used in churches in Seville, for example San Vincente, San Martín and Santa Clara.

A second important centre of tile production emerged during the second half of the sixteenth century at Talavera de la Reina in central Spain. This grew to prominence during the seventeenth century. A Flemish potter, Jan Floris, was active here from 1562 onwards, carrying out commissions for Philip II for royal

The work of the Talavera tile painters can be seen in a remarkable series of panels displayed at Nuestra Señora del Prado, Talavera de la Reina. Panels dating from the sixteenth to the twentieth century can be found both inside and outside the church, which has been described as a veritable *azulejos* museum. Examples range from the enormous tiled altarpieces in the sanctuary, and the narrative scenes in the aisles of the church, to small panels depicting saints and the Virgin Mary, placed on the exterior of the building. Many fine tile pictures can also be seen on either side of the main entrance in the portico, where natural daylight shows the brilliant colours of the tiles in their true splendour.

RIGHT
Panel in the portico of Nuestra Señora del Prado, showing St Anthony as a pilgrim with his pet pig at his feet. Part of an inscription can be seen at the bottom of the panel. In full it reads 'This Church was rebuilt with the aid of God and the townsmen in the years of the Lord 1569 and 1570, Pius V being Pope, and Philip II King of Spain'.

Detail of a tiled Pietà in the portico of Nuestra Señora del Prado. The painter has used a rich yellow-orange to contrast with the shades of blue, and has also managed to convey the sorrow of the Virgin Mary.

Panel dated 1591 depicting the Virgin Mary, on the exterior back wall of Nuestra Señora del Prado, Talavera de la Reina.

OPPOSITE
The old hospital district in Barcelona lies between Mont Taber and Montjuïch. It flourished between the fourteenth and eighteenth centuries, and several original buildings still stand on the Carrer de Hospital. The Santa Cruz hospital is one of these, but is now used for educational purposes. In one of its vestibules, known as the Casa de la Convalecencia, there are well-preserved late seventeenth-century panels of scenes from the life of St Paul, painted by Lorenzo Passoles. Shown here are two adjoining tile panels of the saint and his martyrdom, set in a tiled frame of baroque ornament.

ABOVE LEFT
View of the external portal of the convent church of Santa Paula, Seville, with tiles by Francisco Niculoso and relief roundels by Pedro Millán.

LEFT
Detail of the tiled arch over the portal of the convent church of Santa Paula, Seville. The della Robbia-style tin-glazed roundel by Pedro Millán depicts St Peter and St Paul.

The Salle d'Honneur at Château d'Écouen, near Paris, built for the Constable of France, Anne de Montmorency. The polychrome tin-glazed floor tiles show the Montmorency arms, and were made in the workshop of Masséot Abaquesne in Rouen, *circa* 1542.

Wainscot with blue-and-white tin-glazed tiles in the royal apartments of the monastery of El Escorial, made by the tiler Juan Fernández of Talavera de la Reina between 1570 and 1573. The basic motif is an acanthus leaf. Four tiles are needed to complete the design, which is then repeated. Special border tiles complete the effect. The original contracts, for thousands of tiles, still exist.

buildings in Madrid. Thousands of tiles were also made for Philip II's monastery of El Escorial in the early 1570s by the Talavera tiler Juan Fernández. The rise of Talavera is therefore firmly linked to royal patronage. An unusual collection of locally made tile panels can be found in Nuestra Señora del Prado in Talavera. Over a period of time, figurative tile panels removed from other churches have also been installed there. These cover the walls, both inside and outside, and their subject matter makes up a complex iconographic scheme ranging from the prophets of the Old Testament to scenes from the Life of Christ and the Virgin, and others from the legends of St Anthony and St Christopher.

Barcelona, the capital of Catalonia, is a notable third centre of tile production, which rose to importance from the early seventeenth century onwards. A splendid example of Catalonian tile manufacture can be seen in the old hospital of Santa Cruz. At the entrance to the Casa de la Convalecencia there is a vestibule with magnificent late seventeenth-century tile panels depicting scenes from the life of St Paul. The vestibule leads into a courtyard with green and white tiles on the walls, set above stone benches. Their bold geometrical simplicity complements the semi-circular arches around the courtyard. Barcelona is also known for a type of tile featuring scenes of everyday life, either in blue-and-white or in polychrome on single tiles.

FRANCE

Italian influence extended not only to Spain, but also northwards into France. At the beginning of the sixteenth century a number of potteries came into existence in France that show evidence of contact with Italian methods and designs. Workshops at Lyons and Nevers were followed by others at Rouen, and later at Lisieux and Lille.

The work of Masséot Abaquesne in Rouen, who is recorded between 1526 and 1564, is of considerable importance. Judging from the designs on his tiles it seems likely that he learned from Italians working in France, as his designs follow the Italian fashion for grotesques, which was sweeping France between 1540 and 1580. Abaquesne made paving tiles for Château d'Écouen near Paris, the property of the Constable of France, Anne de Montmorency. The most impressive floor at Écouen is in the Salle d'Honneur, and is decorated with the arms and emblems of de Montmorency. Two tile panels made for the floor of the sacristy of the chapel at Écouen are now preserved at the Musée Condé, Chantilly. They depict two Roman

French tin-glazed border tile with a strapwork pattern, dated 1553.

Panel of polychrome tin-glazed tiles at Château d'Écouen, made *circa* 1550 and attributed to Masséot Abaquesne. One in a series of panels depicting the story of Noah and the Flood.

heroes — one is of Mucius Scaevola plunging his arm into burning coals, the other shows Marcus Curtius leaping on horseback into the chasm opened by an earthquake in the Forum of Rome. The latter incorporates a banner with the inscription '*A Rouen 1542*'. Other commissions, carried out for the Château de la Bâtie d'Urfé, are now in the Louvre, and depict Faith and Justice with various grotesque designs that include a harpy, naked to the waist, terminating in ringlets of ribbons, a device associated with the School of Fontainebleau.

As in most other northern European countries, tin-glazed floor tiles had gone out of fashion in France by the end of the sixteenth century. From then onwards their use was confined to walls. In the seventeenth century tin-glazed wall tiles were made at the factories of Lisieux and Saint-Cloud. Tiles from these centres, together with Dutch tiles, were used to line the six *bassins* in the park of Château de Marly, as well as in the short-lived Trianon de Porcelaine of 1670 at Versailles. These two

schemes were carried out under the patronage of Louis XIV.

French tin-glazed tiles were put to more mundane uses in the eighteenth century, when production was centred in and around Lille, at the factories of Febvrier, Wamps and Masquelier. These tiles were much influenced in design by Dutch examples and were often consciously manufactured '*a la manière de Hollande*'. Tiles were also made throughout the Pas-de-Calais, at Douai, Saint-Omer, Desvres and Saint-Amand-les-Eaux. Some very fine polychrome tiles with Watteau-type landscapes were made at the latter at the end of the eighteenth century.

FLANDERS

The third country where Italian pottery methods stimulated progressive change was Flanders. At the beginning of the sixteenth century, maiolica manufacture moved from Italy to Flanders, and Antwerp became the centre of the new technique. The activities of the Italian potter, Guido di Savino, who came from Castel Durante, were recorded on several occasions. He was certainly well established by 1513 when he bought a house to which, presumably, a workshop was attached. He married a local woman and changed his name to Guido Andries, the name of his father-in-law. The births of several children are recorded, some of whom became potters themselves. Piccolpasso, the author of the *Three Books of the Potter's Art*, was himself a native of Castel Durante and referred to Guido in his work when he wrote 'In Flanders quarried clay is used. I mean at Antwerp, where this art was introduced by one Guido di Savino of this place [Castel Durante] and is still carried on at the present day by his sons'.

LEFT
Four late eighteenth-century tiles, made at the factory of Jean-Baptiste Fauquez in Saint-Amand-les-Eaux. The landscapes show the influence of Watteau. The blue is painted in-glaze (*grand feu*), but the other colours are on-glaze enamels (*petit feu*), therefore two separate glaze firings would have been needed to complete their manufacture.

Guido's workshop must have turned out drug jars, plates, dishes and jugs as well as tiles, as was customary in Italy. His brightly painted wares were evidently in demand, since other local potters such as Frans van Venedigen followed suit. Antwerp tiles were mainly for floors, but single tiles with figurative emblems and house names were used for the facades of buildings facing the street, an example of an early use of the wall tile.

An important maiolica floor which has been ascribed to Guido's workshop can be seen in the chapel of The Vyne, a Tudor mansion at Sherborne St John in Hampshire. The house was built between 1500 and 1520, but the chapel was added later, between 1518 and 1527. The tiles are painted in yellow, blue, orange and green, and are either square, oblong or hexagonal in shape, as were contemporary Italian tiles. The most interesting are those depicting animals or the busts of men and women. Some of the men are shown clean-shaven with long hair cut level at the back of the neck, and wear flat caps with dress true to the fashion of the early sixteenth century. There are also tiles with classical heads wearing laurel wreaths. The tiles show a mixture of Italian and Flemish influences, but the names included in inscriptions on the tiles, such as *LISEBET*, *IASPER* and *MOERIAN*, are of Flemish, not Italian, derivation. Obviously, transporting a moderate number of tiles from Antwerp to the south of England for a patron who had the money to pay for them can have posed no great problem.

A later maiolica floor, for which the commissioning contract has survived, is found at the Abdij (abbey) Herckenrode in Flanders. It was ordered in 1532 from the workshop of Frans van Venedigen. Although no longer *in situ*, surviving fragments show the Italian arrangement

of square tiles with busts of men and women, surrounded by elongated hexagonal tiles decorated with floral ornament. Judging by the kind of patrons who ordered maiolica floors, it would seem that in the sixteenth century only the very rich could afford such luxury. The manufacture of less expensive lead-glazed floor tiles, plain or decorated, continued for common use.

The political troubles that engulfed Antwerp from the 1560s onwards, with the onset of the Eighty Years War between Spain and Holland (Flanders and Holland were Spanish possessions at that time), led to its rapid economic decline. Craftsmen, including maiolica potters, moved to economically more stable and safer places. Some, like Frans Andries and Jan Floris, moved to Spain between 1558 and 1562. Joris Andries moved to Middelburg, Zeeland, in 1564; Adriaen Bogaerd went to Haarlem in

The sixteenth-century maiolica tiles in the chapel at The Vyne, Sherborne St John, Hampshire, are attributed to the workshop of Guido di Savino of Antwerp. A fifteenth-century influence can be seen in the use of the square tile with four hexagonal tiles around it, and in the polychrome rose motifs and other boldly painted foliage. The link with Antwerp, rather than Italy, as had previously been thought, was argued by Bernard Rackham in his *Early Netherlands Maiolica*. He centres his attribution on the fact that the various inscriptions on the tiles are in Flemish, not Italian.

ABOVE LEFT
Detail of the tiles from the chapel at The Vyne. The tile depicting a jester, dressed in green, bears the inscription *SOTGE*, which is Flemish for fool.

OPPOSITE
Group of four early sixteenth-century Flemish tiles from the floor of the chapel at The Vyne. They show busts of women and a man, and a tortoise. The profile head of the man with a crooked nose is supposed to represent Duke Frederico da Montefeltro of Urbino, as he is depicted in the well-known portrait by Piero della Francesca of 1465.

Early seventeenth-century Dutch tile depicting a tulip, with large 'ox-head' motifs in the corners. The use of orange and green shows the influence of Italian maiolica. Tulips were highly prized flowers in Holland at this time, and the bulbs of certain varieties fetched enormous prices. The great interest in the flowers resulted in their depiction in paintings, prints and on tiles.

Jan Vermeer's *A Young Woman Standing at a Virginal* (1671) provides evidence of how tiles were used as a skirting between floor and walls.

Late seventeenth-century Dutch tiles in a small jam cellar at the Paleis Het Loo, Apeldoorn, built for William III and his wife Queen Mary. Landscape tiles, painted in blue with purple borders, are intermixed with purple tiles with geometrical patterns. It is a rare example of the once-rich Dutch tile heritage, little of which now survives.

1566. Jacob Jansen and Jasper Andries travelled to Norwich, in England, in 1567. This movement of skilled potters partly explains the proliferation of the tin-glaze technique throughout Holland and England during the second half of the sixteenth century.

HOLLAND

The centre of manufacture of tin-glazed tiles in northern Europe had now moved from Antwerp to Holland, and their initial use as floor tiles in the Italian fashion had changed to that of wall tiles. However, the reasons why tin-glazed tiles became such a major building component in Dutch architecture in particular at

the beginning of the seventeenth century are complex.

The establishment of pottery workshops in or near towns such as Haarlem, Amsterdam, Rotterdam, Leeuwarden, Harlingen, Utrecht and Delft made tiles much more generally available. The trend for replacing wooden houses with brick-built dwellings gathered apace, particularly in wealthy and expanding cities such as Amsterdam. During the seventeenth century, the wealth created in Holland was shared by a much wider band of the population when compared with other European countries, and a flourishing middle class could afford small, but well-built houses decorated with tiles.

The use of tin-glazed tiles as floor tiles was abandoned because the thin layer of glaze quickly wore off, as many surviving Italian floors demonstrate. Although that may not have mattered to very wealthy patrons who could replace worn tiles whenever needed, it was not the kind of floor covering for the sensible and practical Dutch middle-class consumer. On the wall, however, tiles lasted remarkably well. They were also suitable for fireplaces, where they provided a fireproof surface and helped to reflect heat back into the room, and they were easily cleaned. In cellars they helped to keep out the damp, which so often penetrates walls standing next to the many canals that intersect Dutch towns. Builders found a use for tiles as skirtings, to close gaps between walls and floorboards. Tiles were also used in kitchens and on staircases. Genre painters of the seventeenth century (for example Jan Vermeer and Pieter de Hoogh) show how tiles were used in domestic interiors in their paintings.

Mid-eighteenth-century Dutch tile made in Makkum, Friesland, depicting Christ and the Wise Virgins.

Despite the fact that during the seventeenth century literally millions of tiles were produced for the home market, hardly any examples from that period have survived in their original settings. The reason for this must be sought in the fact that most Dutch tiles were used in the houses of the middle classes. Properties changed hands regularly, and interiors were subjected to constant use and alterations in fashion and technology. The move from open fireplaces to cast-iron stoves, then to central heating is an obvious example. One reason why so many fifteenth-, sixteenth- and seventeenth-century tin-glazed tiles are still found *in situ* in Italy, Spain and Portugal, is that the tilers' patrons there were not housewives, but the church, the court and the aristocracy. Their tiling schemes were often impressive and expensive, and less likely to be changed. The Protestant church in Holland was never a patron of figurative tiling as the Catholic church had been in Portugal or Spain, neither was there a powerful aristocratic group, so the bourgeois middle classes became the tile makers' main customers.

The mania for collecting old Dutch tiles has also contributed to their disappearance from Dutch interiors. This began in the nineteenth century and still continues today. As soon as Dutch tiles became valuable, house owners began to remove them for sale. The few that now remain *in situ* date mainly from the eighteenth or the nineteenth centuries, and are in the countryside rather than in the towns. Fortunately, even before the invention of photography, the appearance of many Dutch interiors had been recorded in paintings, drawings and prints, and such images are invaluable in handing down visual information about settings that often no longer exist. Apart from the

seventeenth- and eighteenth-century Dutch genre painters, particularly good late examples are the watercolours by the artist Mary Ellen Best (1809–91), painted in the 1830s and 1840s in England, Holland and Germany, many of which feature accurately painted tiled interiors.

The increased use of tiles in farmhouses is a phenomenon from the middle of the seventeenth century, and continued well into the nineteenth. By 1650 the Dutch had an excellent infrastructure of canals throughout Holland, thus facilitating the transport of tiles to more isolated localities. Well-to-do farmers installed large fireplaces, or even had some rooms tiled from top to bottom. In the cities, new fashions for wall coverings such as leather or wallpaper had supplanted the use of tiles, but rural communities were slower to respond to such changes. Tiles as an aspect of farmhouse

Interior of a house in Zaandijk, Holland, containing a large mid-eighteenth-century fireplace known as a *smuiger*, a typical feature of many houses in this region. *Smuigers* usually occupy the complete wall area between the floor and the ceiling. This example is decorated with tiles from Amsterdam, painted in purple with biblical scenes. The central panel, however, is from Rotterdam.

architecture were a strong feature in the northern provinces of Holland, particularly Friesland, where tiles were made in bulk by factories in Harlingen, Bolsward and Makkum. These supplied not only the areas in their vicinity, but also exported tiles to rural areas in northern Germany. The factory of Tichelaar, founded in Makkum in 1669, is still active today and has been owned by the same family throughout its history.

Of all the European tin-glazed tiles, single Dutch tiles show the most remarkable diversity of subject matter. Late sixteenth-century and early seventeenth-century Dutch tiles show the influence of Italian maiolica in their colour scheme of blue, orange, green and yellow, and a wide range of designs emerged. The early motifs were tulips, flowerpots, dishes filled with fruit, and a wide range of animals and birds. The importation of Chinese porcelain via the Dutch East India Company at the beginning of the seventeenth century, and the resulting vogue for porcelain led Dutch tile makers to adopt blue and white to the exclusion of all other colours. They also adopted Chinese motifs, although these had more influence on pottery than on tiles. The Chinese influence on Dutch tiles soon faded, but the blue-and-white colour scheme remained. Perhaps the monochrome style was better suited to Calvinist taste.

The range of figurative subject matter increased steadily from 1620 onwards. Tiles with soldiers, ships and scenes from everyday life such as trades and occupations began to appear. By the mid-seventeenth century, the range was extended to include mythological, biblical and rural scenes, peopled by shepherds and shepherdesses, as well as landscapes. Prints, such as the biblical prints issued by Peter Schut

frequently took orders from foreign clients, exporting tiles to France, Germany, Poland, Russia, Portugal and Britain. Its clients were often royalty or aristocrats who had developed a taste for pottery and tiles made in Delft or other Dutch production centres.

When the Dutch stadholder William of Orange ascended the English throne as William III in 1689, he had the French architect Daniel Morot design a dairy for his wife, Mary Stuart, at Hampton Court near London in the early 1690s. This was covered with Dutch tiles made by the Grieksche A factory in Delft, but was demolished soon after Queen Mary's death in 1694. Other important commissions came from France. In 1627 Paul Ardier, defence secretary to Louis XIII, had ordered over 6000 tiles from Holland to be laid on the floor of the portrait gallery in his château at Beauregard in the Loire Valley. They are still *in situ*, and depict soldiers on foot and on horseback, painted in blue-and-white.

The Trianon de Porcelaine at Versailles, which was built for Louis XIV, had Dutch and French tin-glazed tiles used both on the outside and inside walls. Work was completed by 1670, but the building was demolished in 1687 as the tin-glazed tiles used on the exterior proved not to be weatherproof in more northern climes. Another French royal commission was the Pavillon des Bains at Château de Marly, where at the end of the seventeenth century the walls around the baths were lined with Dutch tiles. The building was seriously damaged during the French Revolution, and was finally pulled down in 1810. Excavations have revealed tiles with designs that incorporate the fleur-de-lis and the royal monogram of Louis XIV. Tiles were also put into the Château de Rambouillet between 1715 and 1730 and are still *in situ*.

in Amsterdam in 1659, were often the source for these designs. This vast array of images on single tiles was augmented by various borders and corner motifs. The idea of a single image on an individual tile differs greatly from the vast pictorial schemes, ranging over many tiles, that are to be found in Portugal and Spain. Again, Dutch tiles were used in relatively small domestic interiors, which lent themselves to small designs. This is a further cause of their dispersal – Dutch tiles are attractive to the collector because each tile is complete in itself.

By the seventeenth century, potteries had already begun to specialize in the production of tiles, rather than have a mixed output of tiles and household wares, as had been common practice. Tile factories came into being which were capable of a large, sustained production. The eighteenth-century factory of Jan Aalmis, De Bloempot, in Rotterdam, is a case in point. It

ABOVE
The kitchen of the Jagdschloss Amalienburg, built by François Cuvilliés between 1734 and 1739 in the park of Schloss Nymphenburg near Munich, is richly decorated with Dutch tiles. These include large flower panels, similar to the examples found at Rambouillet.

RIGHT
The Pagodenburg, built by Joseph Effner between 1716 and 1719 in the park of Schloss Nymphenburg, has an exquisite octagonal room where blue-and-white Dutch landscape tiles have been used superbly as part of the overall interior decoration.

The true magnificence of Dutch painted tiles can be fully appreciated in the eighteenth-century Schloss Falkenlust, Brühl, in Germany, built for Prince Clemens August between 1729 and 1737. Tiles decorate both staircases and rooms, harmonizing with the rococo interior, which was designed by the architect François Cuvilliés. The tiles shown here were made by the De Bloempot factory in Rotterdam. The painted roundels depict herons being hunted with falcons.

Despite the destruction of the Second World War, Germany can still boast some spectacular palaces and castles that have extensive Dutch tiling schemes, still in their original locations. A tiled kitchen with large panels of flower vases as well as many individual landscape tiles can still be seen at the Jagdschloss Amalienburg (hunting lodge) in the park at Schloss Nymphenburg near Munich, which was erected between 1734 and 1739. Function is combined here with opulent splendour. At Brühl there are two castles, Schloss Falkenlust and Augustusburg; both have extensive areas of Dutch tiles on the walls of rooms and staircases. Their flower vase and figurative panels were made in Rotterdam and installed in the 1730s. A large tiled hall of *circa* 1720 can be found at Schloss Caputh, Potsdam, near Berlin. It is covered with thousands of individual tiles showing landscapes, ships and children's games.

The late eighteenth century was a difficult time for the Dutch tin-glaze industry, with both pottery and tiles experiencing a drop in demand. The increasing fashion for wallpaper, the effect upon trade of the Napoleonic wars, and the rise in popularity of Staffordshire tableware affected the demand for pottery wares of all types, and coupled with new production techniques invented in England, had sometimes catastrophic effects. Relatively few Dutch tin-glaze factories survived into the nineteenth century.

OPPOSITE
During the first quarter of the eighteenth century, the Comte de Toulouse carried out extensive renovations at the château of Rambouillet. One room, the *cabinet des bains*, had its walls covered with Dutch tiles, including sumptuous polychrome flower panels, surrounded by finely painted landscape tiles.

ABOVE
Tiled room in the Menshikov Palace,
St Petersburg. In the corner is an early
eighteenth-century stove, of Russian
manufacture, while the walls and ceiling are
covered with Dutch early eighteenth-
century tiles. Those on the ceiling are held
in place with copper pins.

RIGHT
The kitchen of the eighteenth-century
Summer Palace in St Petersburg. The tiles
are either Dutch imports, or were made by
Russian potters who had Dutch training. The
design is a traditional Dutch pattern known
as 'Jeruzalemveren' (Jerusalem leaves).

PORTUGAL

The tile culture of the Portuguese *azulejos* is something that no visitor to Portugal can fail to notice. Tiles are used with an exuberance that is matched nowhere else in Europe.

The Portuguese absorbed many ideas from Spain, Flanders and Holland in their tile production, and during the first half of the sixteenth century, most tiles were imported from Seville. *Cuenca* and *cuerda seca* tiles were used in the Palácio Nacional de Sintra on walls, around door frames, and for courtyard benches. They were also used extensively on the walls and columns in the Sé Velha (old cathedral) at Coimbra. Painted Spanish tiles were in vogue during the second half of the sixteenth century, as can be seen in the Jesuit church of São Roque in Lisbon, where 'diamond point' pattern tiles, which were very common in Seville and Valencia, cover the interior walls.

Native Portuguese tile production began in Lisbon during the third quarter of the sixteenth century, and the influence of the Italo-Flemish style, either from Valencia or directly from Flanders, is evident. A splendid example of this is the tiling executed by Francisco de Matos in 1584 for the Capela de São Roque in the Jesuit church of the same name in Lisbon. Renaissance-style festoons and vases, and Flemish *ferronie* ornament are combined with more naturalistic scenes from the life of St Roque. Tiles in simple chequer-board arrangements were also used at this time. Square or rectangular tiles set at oblique angles on walls resulted in dynamic, energetic rhythms, sometimes combined with painted abstract motifs. An example can be seen in the small lower cloister adjacent to the church of Madre-de-Deus in Lisbon, where tiles and architecture are particularly well integrated.

RIGHT
Panel depicting the personification of the River Euphrates in the loggia of the Quinta da Bacalhoa (Bacalhoa manor house) in Azeitão, Portugal. It dates from *circa* 1570, and was clearly influenced by Flemish mannerism.

Large Dutch tile panel, showing hermits in a
landscape, in the convent church of Madre-
de-Deus, Lisbon. Made by Jan van Oort in
Amsterdam, it was installed in 1698.

View of the arcaded small lower cloister in
the convent of Madre-de-Deus, Lisbon.
Early seventeenth-century Portuguese tiles
grace the walls.

The church and convent complex of Madre-de-Deus, at Xabregas in Lisbon, now houses the Portuguese national tile collection. The Museu Nacional do Azulejo, as it is known, contains a magnificent display of loose panels and tiles, but the convent buildings themselves also contain an impressive number of tiles *in situ*. Madre-de-Deus was founded in 1509 by the Dowager Dona Leonor, the sister of King Manuel I, and was enlarged and embellished throughout the seventeenth and eighteenth centuries. In the baroque convent church, enormous tile panels made in Amsterdam in 1698 decorate the walls, while Portuguese tiles were used extensively in the various cloisters.

During the seventeenth century, Portuguese tiles were widely used in churches and palaces. The fashion for polychromatic decoration changed to one of solely blue-and-white at the end of the seventeenth century, mainly under the influence of Dutch tiles. These were imported in great quantities, and the vogue for them forced Portuguese tile producers to follow suit. During the eighteenth century vast murals of blue-and-white tiles covered buildings from top to bottom, including sometimes the ceiling. The church of Mercês in Lisbon has an astounding tiled ceiling, with baroque decorative details framing figurative scenes that were painted by António de Oliveira Bernardes *circa* 1714. The entrance hall of the Monastery of São Vicente de Fora has large areas of tiles with baroque decorations, framing panels depicting the Portuguese kings and various battle scenes, painted by Manuel dos Santos *circa* 1710, all again in blue-and-white. These vast and most impressive schemes have the effect of de-materializing the walls, and change one's perception of the interior space of the building.

It seems strange that the Dutch, who did not produce monumental tiling schemes for the home market, managed to compete so successfully with native Portuguese workshops. Some of the biggest tile schemes ever undertaken by workshops in Amsterdam and Rotterdam were produced for churches and palaces in Portugal. Jan van Oort, an Amsterdam tile maker, made panels depicting scenes from the life of St Teresa of Avila for the church of Nossa Senhora, Conceição dos Cardais, Lisbon, *circa* 1698, while either the Rotterdam tile painter Cornelis Boumeester, or the Amsterdam tile manufacturer Willem van der Kloet, made panels depicting views of different European cities for

RIGHT
The Salao Nobre in the Palácio dos Condes de Anadia, Mangualde, near Viseu, Portugal. The walls are covered with blue-and-white tiles of *circa* 1730.

ABOVE

The convent church of Lóios at Arraiolos in central
Portugal is a good example of Portuguese blue-and-
white figurative and decorative tiling. The various
religious scenes were painted by Gabriel del Barco in
1700.

RIGHT

The gardens of the Palácio Nacional de Queluz
contain the extraordinary Lago Grande, a section of
the Jamor stream which was converted into a tiled
canal where the royal family could enjoy boating
expeditions. One of the most extravagant pieces of
tiled architecture in Portugal, it was built between
1755 and 1756, and can be filled with water via
sluices at either end.

Panel from the tiled balustrade of a staircase in the garden of the Palácio Pombal in Oeiras, near Lisbon. It dates from between 1760 and 1770, and is decorated with a hunting scene painted in purple, within a polychrome rococo border.

the Paço Saldanha (now the Palácio da Ega) in Lisbon *circa* 1715. The largest Dutch tile panels ever made were installed at the end of the seventeenth century in the church of the convent of Madre-de-Deus, Xabregas, in Lisbon.

Following the Lisbon earthquake of 1755, many parts of the city had to be rebuilt. Tiles were used on a large scale because they were recognized as a finishing material that was long-lasting, hygienic and decorative. The faience pottery and tiles of the Real Fábrica do Rato, the royal tile factory, which opened in 1767, helped to strengthen the acceptance of the rococo style. Although blue-and-white was still popular, colours began to be used again, mainly yellow and purple. Such polychrome schemes in the rococo style can be seen on the exterior walls of the Palácio Pombal in Oeiras, dated 1767, and at the Sala das Mangas at the

royal palace in Queluz, where large polychrome scenes were painted in 1784 by Francisco Jorge da Costa. In the garden at Queluz, an extraordinary tiled canal was built in 1755 for boating expeditions by the royal family. Tiles became an important feature in Portuguese garden design during the second half of the eighteenth century, and tiled garden staircases, benches, fountains and ponds with tiled surrounds were much in fashion.

The Napoleonic invasion of Portugal in 1807 forced the royal family to flee to Brazil, and the ensuing war and economic upheavals seriously affected tile production. Even with the return of the royal family in 1821, the internal political situation remained unstable, and it was not until the second half of the nineteenth century that the manufacture of tiles once more became a major industry.

OPPOSITE
The Palácio de Fronteira at Benfica near Lisbon has many fine examples of tiled garden architecture. The Galeria dos Reis (Gallery of the Kings) is a stepped terrace built *circa* 1670, overlooking a narrow strip of water. On the lowest level there are round-headed, tiled panels depicting the ancestors of the palace's builders, the Mascarenhas family, on horseback. At the upper level is a balustraded terrace, where busts of kings are displayed in tiled niches. The unusual tinglazed tiles have embossed decorations painted in blue and copper lustre.

BRITAIN

Dutch influence dominated the production of tiles in northern Europe. In Britain tin-glazed tiles had been made in small quantities from the late sixteenth century onwards, but this had always been a minor industry, overshadowed by the huge Dutch output. However, Flemish and Dutch potters did come to Britain to set up workshops, and passed on their skills to native potters. Jasper Andries and Jacob Jansen moved from Antwerp to Norwich in 1567, and three years later Jansen was in London, where he petitioned Elizabeth I to be allowed to make tin-glazed pottery and tiles. The tin-glazed pottery industry was well established in London by this date, with potteries at Aldgate, Southwark and Lambeth. English finds of surviving early seventeenth-century polychrome tiles have come mainly from excavations in London, but there is some dispute as to whether they were made there by Dutch potters, or were imported from Holland.

When taking a broad view of developments in Britain, the period of greatest interest is the eighteenth century, when the main centres of production were London, Bristol, Liverpool and Glasgow. Until the middle of the eighteenth century, English tiles, decorated with biblical and landscape subjects, closely followed the designs of their Dutch prototypes. After 1750 English tiles developed a more individual character, which can be seen in unusual edgings such as the 'bianco-sopra-bianco' border, often found on Bristol tiles, or in finely painted chinoiserie figures and birds in blue, yellow, orange, purple and green. Corner motifs also began to diverge from Dutch examples, and took on a peculiarly English character.

Contemporary newspaper advertisements for pottery sometimes record the range of wares produced. Tiles are mentioned in an advertisement placed by the Delftfield pottery in the Glasgow *Courant* for the 2–9 May 1757. Among many different delftware products, 'chimney-tiles' are mentioned, indicating where they were to be used. Most English tin-glazed tiles were used in fireplaces, for the same reasons as they were in Holland. At times they were also used to tile alcoves housing wash-basins, in larders and pantries, or in dairies. Occasionally small panels were used as exterior signs for inns or coffee shops.

The output of tiles in Britain during this period was relatively small. There were no specialist factories and the production of tiles was always secondary to the manufacture of other wares. During the second half of the eighteenth century, the industry fell victim to

The larder (now demolished) from Shide House, Newport, Isle of Wight, decorated with eighteenth-century English delftware tiles. A few Dutch tiles have found their way among them. It seems likely that the original layout of the tiles was altered, and that the installation shown here was of a nineteenth-century date.

SWITZERLAND, AUSTRIA AND GERMANY

In Central Europe, the manufacture of a particular type of tile, the stove tile, developed from the fifteenth century onwards. It sprang from the need to have a secure and sustained form of heating during the long winters. Stove tiles are different from floor and wall tiles, being very thick and heavy, in order to help them retain and radiate heat. The stoves themselves were freestanding, usually placed in the corner of a room, and could be over 2.5 metres high. The main production centres during the sixteenth, seventeenth and eighteenth centuries were in Switzerland, Austria and Germany, but they were also made in Russia and Sweden.

Many such tiles were made at Winterthur in central Switzerland, where their manufacture became a distinct craft, dominated by several generations of the Pfau family. Swiss stove tiles of the sixteenth to eighteenth centuries were often covered with white tin glaze and painted in polychrome with complex figurative scenes and inscriptions. A magnificent example is still *in situ* in a panelled room at the former Chancellery of the Freuler Palace, Nafels, made by Hans Pfau II. In Austria during the same period stove tiles were made at Innsbruck by the Gantner family, at nearby Kitzbühel, and were also manufactured at Bozen (now Bolzano, Italy). Bartholomaus Dill was active in Bozen *circa* 1526, and painted stove tiles with scenes of the heroic deeds of Jason, Samson and Hercules, based on the prints of Hans Burgkmair.

German stove tile production was centred in Nuremberg. Rather than using the maiolica technique, they were made with figurative scenes and decorations in high relief, covered with green or brown-black glazes. The relief surface also had a direct practical function, as it

new techniques and production methods, as the development of transfer printing made it a serious rival to the practice of painting tiles and pottery by hand. New kinds of stoneware and china clay bodies were made, which were harder and more durable than tin-glazed ware. Staffordshire ceramics, with Wedgwood in the lead, pioneered the transformation of the British pottery industry. Potteries making tin-glazed ware had the choice of changing to the manufacture of new products or of being forced out of business, and none of the British tin-glaze potteries survived into the nineteenth century.

LEFT
Group of six English delftware tiles, probably from Bristol, dated between 1725 and 1750. Their central designs are based on K'ang-hsi porcelain, but the corner motifs of winged cherubs are thoroughly European.

Eighteenth-century stove with tin-glazed tiles and painted floral decoration at Stureholm, Sweden.

style to the Dutch models. However, this never developed into a sustained tradition. The output was relatively small, and could never match the quality of the best Dutch products.

German tin-glazed tiles were essentially for the houses and palaces of the wealthy. They were used on walls, or on the square pillars that supported ceiling vaults, and occasionally for the risers of staircases. The colours were mainly traditional blue-and-white, with the occasional addition of purple. Some of the more interesting tiles from the Dorotheenthal factory are decorated with idyllic scenes painted in purple within a green border, and tiles from the Ansbach factory feature birds, ships, hunters and figures in landscapes, exquisitely painted using a full palette of green, yellow, blue and purple.

Methods of using tiles on walls differed greatly. Sometimes whole walls were tiled, as for example at Schloss Favorite near Rastatt.

RIGHT
Ceramic stove of *circa* 1500 in the Golden Room (1495–1519) at Hohensalzburg, Austria, built for Archbishop Leonhard von Keutschach. The polychrome tin-glazed relief tiles depict saints and religious scenes.

increased the surface area and thus the heat radiation of the tiles. As in Switzerland and Austria, stove tile manufacture in Germany was a specialist craft. This is emphasized by the distinction made in the German language between stove tiles and wall or floor tiles. The former are known as *kacheln* (*kachel* in German means stove tile), the latter as *fliesen*.

The production of tin-glazed wall tiles in Germany took place mainly in the eighteenth century, when a number of factories were set up throughout the country to produce pottery and tiles in direct competition with the Dutch. Dresden, Frankfurt, Ansbach, Dorotheenthal and Kellinghusen near the Danish border are examples of the places where these potteries were founded. The Germans usually relied on Dutch potters for initial help and guidance, and some good tiles were made, but in a different

Mid-eighteenth-century Danish tin-glazed, relief-moulded tiles, *in situ* in a private residence in Borreby, Sjaelland, in Denmark. They were made by the Store Kongensgade factory, Copenhagen. These unusual tiles are found only in Denmark.

A more refined and sensitive use can be seen in the rococo interiors of certain German palaces such as Hirschberg, where narrow, vertical strips of tiling in frames accentuate certain parts of the room, while the remaining spaces are given over to wall paintings or decorative plasterwork.

DENMARK

Factories in Denmark were usually led by German-trained potters. The Danish king Frederick IV encouraged one Johann Wolff to come and work at Frederiksbergslot in 1721, and for a short period some pottery was made there, but production terminated in 1722. In 1723 the Store Kongensgade factory was established in Copenhagen with Wolff in charge. Pottery and tiles were made under the name of 'Delfs Porcelin og Hollandsch Steentøy', which clearly indicates an intention to create products in the Dutch manner. In 1725 Wolff went to Sweden to start a factory, and a certain Johann Pfau from Lübeck took over the running of Store Kongensgade. Blue-and-white tiles made for the small, luxury 'Prinsessernes Pandekage-køkken' (Pancake kitchen of the princesses) in Frederiksbergslot in 1735 can still be seen in their original position. The Store Kongensgade factory also made some very unusual tiles which can be regarded as uniquely Danish. Some have a relief border and painted central motifs, while others were completely moulded in relief and covered with a white tin glaze.

Another Copenhagen factory was the Blåtårns Ovnfabrik, which was active between 1738 and 1754, while on the island of Amager the Castrup Werk made tiles during the second half of the eighteenth century.

The tiles in the dining room of the Residenz in Ansbach, Germany, were installed in 1763. They were made locally by the Ansbach pottery, which was active from 1710 to 1804, and show a great diversity of subject matter, including animals, birds, hunting scenes and landscapes, as well as oriental scenes, such as the finely painted example illustrated above. The dominant colours are yellow, purple, green and blue, and the corners of the tiles are decorated with quarter rosettes, which form whole flowers when four tiles are set together.

Late nineteenth-century Dutch landscape tile, by the firm of van Hulst in Harlingen. It was made in a six-inch format for export to Britain, where it was used in a cast-iron fireplace.

Late nineteenth-century Dutch tiles in a bathroom at Pownall Hall, Wilmslow, in Cheshire. This strong decorative design, where floral motifs alternate with a chequer-board pattern, appealed to Arts and Crafts taste.

OPPOSITE
The kitchen of Monet's house at Giverny, where the artist lived from 1883 to his death in 1926. The walls are decorated with an assortment of nineteenth-century French tin-glazed tiles.

LATE TIN-GLAZED TILES IN FRANCE, SPAIN, PORTUGAL AND HOLLAND

By the end of the eighteenth century, the manufacture of tin-glazed wall tiles had virtually ceased in Britain, and declined to a considerable extent in Germany and France. Production continued in Spain, Portugal and Holland, where it had always been an important part of the economy. In the nineteenth century tiles were no longer the exclusive preserve of the wealthy and the aristocracy, and acquired more mundane uses, both functional and decorative. The main market remained domestic, but tiles were also used in the form of picture panels for public places.

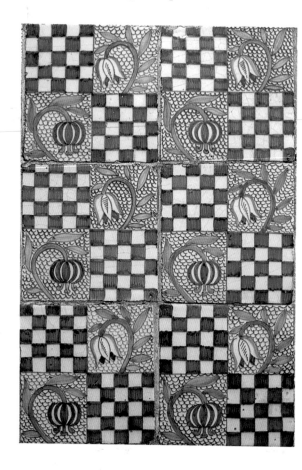

In France the firm of Fourmaintraux was founded in Desvres in 1804, and established itself as a major producer of tin-glazed tiles. It is still active today. Similarly, manufacturers at Ponchon and Saint-Paul near Beauvais made hand-painted tiles. In an attempt to match the production of industrially manufactured tiles, stencil decoration, which was less time-consuming than hand painting, was developed. Mainly abstract stencilled designs could be applied to tiles with great effect. The kitchen of Monet's house at Giverny has tiling of this kind.

The tradition of hand-painted tiles continued in Spain in the nineteenth and twentieth centuries, in major production centres such as Seville, Valencia, Barcelona and Talavera de la Reina. Tile panels with devotional images of Christ, the Virgin and various saints, created for the exteriors of houses, public buildings and churches, are one manifestation of this and are still popular today. These tile panels were frequently made by the Santa Ana tile factory in Triana, Seville, which was founded in 1870, and can be seen throughout southern Spain.

Following the end of the Napoleonic wars and the initial internal economic turmoil, the Portuguese tile industry revived, with the establishment of new factories in Lisbon. The Constância factory was founded in 1836, the Lamego factory in 1849, and the Sacavém factory in 1850. The use of tiles to cover the facades of buildings, a form of decoration first used on a large scale in Brazil, was an important factor in this revival. Tiles used in this way also had a direct practical function, as they reflected back the heat from the sun. These facades are one of the most interesting manifestations of the joint aesthetic and practical values of tiles, and are still a feature of much Portuguese domestic and public architecture today.

ABOVE
Panel of Art Nouveau tin-glazed tiles from a shop front in Lisbon.

LEFT
The 1865 facade of the Viúva Lamego tile factory in Largo do Intendente, Lisbon, painted by Ferreira das Tabuletas.

RIGHT
Detail of a panel from the facade of the Lamego tile factory. The Chinaman holds a scroll bearing the factory's name.

Despite severe cut-backs in the tin-glaze industry at the end of the eighteenth century, a few Dutch firms managed to survive into the nineteenth and twentieth centuries. The Bloempot factory in Rotterdam was the only surviving tilery of a once flourishing industry, and went into liquidation itself shortly after the middle of the nineteenth century. A new tile factory was set up in 1851 by J.F. Kleyn in Delfshaven near Rotterdam, under the name Piet Hein, but it too ceased trading in 1866. Tile production in Friesland fared slightly better. The Tichelaar factory at Makkum, and van Hulst and Tjallingii in Harlingen, still found customers in rural areas and exported their wares to northern Germany and Denmark.

In the Dutch town of Utrecht there was even a minor revival in tile production. Two new factories were founded: Ravesteyn in 1845 and Schillemans in 1856, who supplied tiles to rural areas around Utrecht. Ravesteyn and van Hulst also exported tiles to Britain. The vogue for handmade Dutch tiles, encouraged by the Arts and Crafts movement, led to the production of special tiles for the British market. The firm of Morris & Company even had tiles made by Ravesteyn from their own designs. A new fashion provided a further outlet for tiles as they began to be used in porches and under eaves. Many examples survive on the fronts of buildings throughout Holland.

One of the reasons for continued tin-glaze tile manufacture in these countries was the fact that for the greater part of the nineteenth century, the Industrial Revolution passed them by. Countries in the forefront of that revolution, notably Britain, enjoyed a revival in their own ceramics industries, which included the mass production of machine-made tiles from the mid-nineteenth century onwards.

Tiles in the back kitchen of a Betuwe farmhouse from Varik. The farmhouse was taken down brick-by-brick at its original location, and rebuilt at the open-air museum in Arnhem. The building dates back to the seventeenth century, but has been continuously altered and extended. The large back kitchen, with its splendid display of purple flower-vase tiles, dates from *circa* 1900. The tiles cover not only the walls but also the box-bed in the corner, no doubt placed in that position to take advantage of the warmth from the nearby stove.

The dining room of Epema State, a house at Ysbrechtum, Friesland, in Holland. The fireplace tiles are replicas, based on early seventeenth-century examples, and were made by van Hulst in Harlingen in 1894.

3

THE MARCH OF
THE MACHINE

The Industrial Revolution had far-reaching implications for the manufacture, decoration and use of tiles. The development of new machines and manufacturing techniques meant greater and faster production of goods, with machines and mechanical processes replacing hand work. In this, British entrepreneurs, such as the tile manufacturer Herbert Minton, led the way. In the second half of the nineteenth century, British technology spread throughout Europe. Machine processes pioneered in Britain were rapidly adopted by the tile industries in Germany, France and Belgium, and eventually reached Holland, Spain and Portugal as well, where traditional tile-making techniques still lingered.

Panel of unglazed
encaustic floor tiles
with classical motifs,
made by Minton,
Hollins & Company
circa 1865. A type of
tile often used in
civic buildings such
as town halls.

On-glaze, transfer-printed English delftware tile, dated between 1757 and 1761, decorated with a picturesque classical landscape. Signed in the bottom right corner 'J. Sadler Liverpool'.

MECHANIZED TILE PRODUCTION IN BRITAIN

In Britain, industrial processes that replaced traditional craft techniques were developed for the first time. An early example of this is the transfer printing of pottery and tiles by the Liverpool printer John Sadler. Sadler had set up his own printing works in Harrington Street, Liverpool, in 1748, where he experimented with transfer printing on ceramics. By 1756 he had mastered the process sufficiently well to begin commercial production. In an affidavit dated 2 August 1756, he took oath that he and his partner, Guy Green, 'without the aid or assistance of any person or persons, did, within the space of six hours, to wit, betwixt the hours of nine in the morning and three in the afternoon of the same day, print upwards of twelve hundred earthenware tiles of different patterns, at Liverpoole aforesaid, and which, as these deponents have heard and believe, were more in number and better and neater, than one hundred skilful pot painters could have painted in the like space of time in the common and usual way painting with pencil' (that is, a fine brush). In many ways this statement points up the central concerns of the mechanical process: faster, better, cheaper and increased production. Here, the saving in labour costs was particularly significant. Sadler was not the actual inventor of transfer printing on pottery, but he demonstrated its early potential for use on tiles. Even Wedgwood made use of Sadler's expertise in the early days of his firm, and sent pottery to Liverpool to be printed, before it became common practice for this activity to be carried out at the potteries themselves.

The technique of transfer printing used either a transfer paper or a thin sheet of firm gelatine (the glue-bat method) to transfer an image from an inked engraving plate to the ceramic surface. In the former, plate and transfer paper were run through a printing press, and the transfer paper, printed with the image, would then be rubbed by hand onto the pot or tile. In the glue-bat method the gelatine readily picked up the oily ink on contact with the engraved surface of the plate, and no printing press was needed.

Sadler quickly began to specialize in printing designs onto blank white tin-glazed tiles, commonly available in Liverpool at this time, using ceramic enamel colours mixed with ink. These on-glaze colours could be fired onto the glazed surface of the tile at the relatively low temperatures of a muffle kiln. (Muffle kilns are designed for the firing of delicate glazes and on-glaze decorations, and have interiors completely shielded from direct contact with flames and gasses – only the heat enters the kiln interior.) Transfer printing rapidly became one of the most widely used methods of decorating ceramics. However, on-glaze decoration was vulnerable to wear, and was not suitable for tableware, or for tiles in areas that saw heavy use. The printed image had to go under a transparent glaze for protection, but the technical implications of this were problematic. Printing under the glaze meant firing the ceramic colours at the same temperature as the glaze, that is 1000°C or over, and few colours could withstand such fierce heat. An exception was a blue made from cobalt oxide, which proved very suitable for this practice.

Experiments in underglaze printing were linked to the search for better types of ceramic bodies. Until the mid-eighteenth century, the earthenware body of red or yellow firing clay had been hidden by an opaque white tin glaze, but the need for better-quality ceramic bodies

that could be covered with transparent glazes was increasing, and ultimately resulted in the development, by Wedgwood and Spode, of creamware and pearlware. Underglaze transfer printing also became possible; Josiah Spode had managed this successfully by 1784, and blue-and-white underglaze transfer-printed pottery became immensely popular as a cheaper alternative to blue-and-white delftware and Chinese porcelain.

With the demise of tin-glaze pottery manufacture, the early transfer-printed Liverpool 'delftware' tiles also disappeared. Some printed creamware tiles were made, and a small number of tiles were also produced by Spode and Copeland with transfer-printed designs in blue under the glaze, but relatively few tiles were made in Britain during the late eighteenth and early nineteenth century.

The man who laid the foundation for nineteenth-century machine production of tiles was Herbert Minton. Two parallel stories unfold here, the manufacture of floor tiles based on the patent of Samuel Wright, and the machine production of wall tiles developed from the patent of Richard Prosser.

In 1835 Minton had bought a share in a patent developed by Samuel Wright of Shelton, for the manufacture of inlaid or encaustic floor tiles. Wright had patented his invention for the 'manufacture of ornamental tiles, bricks and quarries for floors, pavements and other purposes' in 1830, and had hoped to make tiles for the domestic market. He had perfected the technique of inlaying one clay into another and must have fulfilled some orders, as his products were mentioned and praised in Loudon's *Encyclopaedia of Cottage, Farm and Villa Architecture* of 1833. However, the demand for his product cannot have been great since in 1835 he

Minton unglazed encaustic tile *circa* 1860, depicting the stigmata.

disposed of the patent to Herbert Minton and Walter Chamberlain on a ten per cent royalty basis. Minton must also have acquired Wright's old stock of tiles, which were of a buff colour with a black inlay, as he was able to supply some to Kilmory Castle at Lochgilphead in Argyll in 1837, where they are still *in situ*.

Wright used metal or plaster moulds, and presumably a screw press to force the clay down into them. The moulds had a design standing up in relief at the bottom of them and when the tile came out of the mould, the pattern was indented into the clay. The sunken areas of the design were filled with different coloured clay, which was then scraped level, and the tile left to dry before firing. The problems that had to be overcome were mainly to find suitable clays that contracted at a similar rate. If the inlaid clay shrank more than the body of the tile, it would fall out, but if it did not shrink as fast as the body, the tile would crack during firing. It is ironic that a medieval process was here being revived.

Minton and Chamberlain conducted further trials at their works with red tile bodies and a white inlay, in imitation of medieval tiles. They soon realised that it was in the ecclesiastical market, and not the domestic one, that the demand for their tiles lay. Their early products were thus intended for use in churches, and the designs came from medieval examples that had been collected, recorded and published by interested architects and antiquarians such as L. N. Cottingham, H. Eginton and A. W. N. Pugin; all of whom were involved in Gothic revival architecture or the restoration of medieval churches.

Chamberlain, who ran the Worcester Porcelain Company, must be given the credit for bringing encaustic tiles for church use on to the market before Minton. In 1837 he supplied tiles for the floor of Holy Trinity Church in Stratford-upon-Avon, but Chamberlain's products were not as well made as Minton's, and he failed to develop colour combinations beyond brown and yellow. He was never given the prestige commissions that Minton eventually obtained, and by 1848 tile making had ceased at Worcester.

The discovery of the well-preserved medieval tiled floor of the Westminster Abbey Chapterhouse, hidden under a temporary wooden floor since the Dissolution of the Monasteries, caused great excitement. Cottingham recorded the tiles in 1841, and Minton made copies of them for the Temple Church in London, which was then being restored. By 1842 this, the first of Minton's great church commissions, was in place. In the same year Minton brought out a printed catalogue entitled *Examples of Old English Tiles*, which included all the Westminster Abbey Chapter-

Minton inlaid floor tiles at Temple Church, London, dated 1842. Originally in the nave, they were relaid in the upper gallery of the rotunda during the restoration of war damage after 1945. They show the Pascal Lamb, which is the emblem of the Middle Temple. The inlaid section of the design has been overpainted with yellow ceramic enamel, a particular feature of many early examples of this type of Minton tile.

house patterns, and from that date the floor tile business went from strength to strength. Moreover, shortly after 1842, Minton increased the colour range of his encaustics and introduced blue and green alongside the conventional brown-red and yellow. The manufacture of visually much more striking pavements was now possible.

Minton's involvement with the great Gothic revival architect A. W. N. Pugin was particularly important, as Pugin used Minton floor tiles, decorated with his own designs, in most of his buildings. Perhaps the most notable commission to arise out of this association was the paving of the Palace of Westminster with encaustic tiles designed by Pugin. The first tiles were in place in 1847, but work continued for

LEFT
Tiles bearing the personal monogram and heraldic emblem of A. W. N. Pugin, on the floor of his private chapel at The Grange, Ramsgate, where he went to live in 1841.

several years. Encaustic tiles were also made for Queen Victoria's Isle of Wight home, Osborne House, which was built between 1845 and 1850. During the 1860s and 1870s there was an unprecedented demand for floor tiles for use in public buildings. The floor of St George's Hall, Liverpool (1852), is one of the most magnificent in Britain, and orders for other town halls such as Leeds and Rochdale followed.

Meanwhile, Minton also developed wall tile production. In 1840 Richard Prosser had invented a method of making small articles such as buttons and tesserae by compressing dust clay in a screw press. (Dust clay is specially prepared clay that has been milled to a very fine powder and then slightly moistened.) Minton adapted this method to wall tile production, and large fly-wheel presses were constructed to manufacture tiles to a standard size of six inches square. The advantages of tiles made from dust clay are that they need less time to dry, do not shrink so much and are not likely to warp during firing. They have a perfectly

smooth surface on which it is possible to print or execute other decorations. For plain tiles, metal dies with flat bottoms were used, but it was also possible to make relief tiles in one and the same operation by using dies with relief designs. These processes allowed for mass production of tiles of a consistent quality at affordable prices, and tiles with machine-moulded designs covered with translucent or opaque glazes became a major and relatively inexpensive product for architectural use.

Printing methods were modified continuously. Minton took advantage of an invention of two printers, Collins and Reynolds, of 1848, which made it possible to print areas of flat colour, and adapted this to printing on tiles. It was essentially a form of lithography, which depends on the repellent action between water and greasy ink, and is carried out on a flat stone slab or metal block. It enabled different colours to be printed at the same time, and Pugin designed tiles in several colours for this technique, early examples of which can be found in

Set of twelve underglaze transfer-printed tiles of Aesop's *Fables*. Designed by John Moyr Smith for Mintons China Works, *circa* 1875.

fireplaces at the Palace of Westminster. Monochrome prints were also made by this method. The tile designer John Moyr Smith used monochrome prints for several series of tiles, including his scenes from Shakespeare, the Old and New Testaments and Aesop's Fables.

Printing from engraved plates was relatively slow, so improvements were made to speed up this process, including the use of engraved rollers in the printing press from which large numbers of impressions could be taken. However, the printing of colour remained difficult for some time and transfer-printed tiles were often coloured in by hand.

Another convenient method of decorating tiles quickly was the use of an airbrush attached to an air-pump. This could spray glazes or ceramic colour through stencils onto tiles. Maw and Wedgwood also experimented with using photographic images to decorate tiles, but it was the photographer George Henry Grundy in Derby who achieved the greatest success. He produced tiles with photographic images held under the glaze, which made them very durable. His method consisted of coating a photographic plate with ceramic colour, then printing it directly onto the dust-pressed tile blank. After a first hardening-on firing, the tile was dipped into clear glaze and fired again. Grundy was granted a patent in 1896. Photographic tiles with views of towns, abbeys and churches proved to be most popular.

Increased mechanization and steam power were changing the tile industry, and the raw clay came to be processed more and more by machines, including blungers for mixing clay, clay slip agitators, pug mills for plastic clay, clay pulverizers for making dust clay, and tile presses. Kilns were improved with regard to their structure, but above all in their devices for measuring heat. In the late eighteenth century Wedgwood had pioneered a pyrometer, designed to make the outcome of firings more accurate. This device was based on the principle that clay contracts in its dimension as it is exposed to progressively higher temperatures. Another device, developed in the nineteenth century, was Watkin's heat recorder. This was an oblong block of hard ceramic, with circular recesses in which pellets of ceramic compositions with known melting points were placed. These devices were positioned in the kiln where they could be observed through spy holes, and ensured that more accurate judgements could be made on the progress of the firing, and most importantly, the point at which to halt it. Since the firing is the final stage in the tile-making process and the success of all the work done until that point depends upon its outcome, these advances in heat measuring technology were vital.

Specialization within the industry developed at the same time. The practice had been for glazes and ceramic colours to be prepared 'in-house' at each pottery, but from 1870 onwards the firm of A. F. Wenger at Stoke-on-Trent began to supply ready-made glazes and colours, not only in Britain but also abroad. These developments allowed for the establishment of a new type of firm – the specialist tile decorator. W. B. Simpson and Sons in London or the Decorative Art Tile Company Ltd in Stoke-on-Trent could buy dust-pressed tiles from larger firms such as Maw or Minton and ready-made glazes from Wenger.

The machines and technical innovations of the nineteenth century transformed earlier techniques of tile making. Handmade and hand-decorated tiles had showed diversity in their form and decoration, with no two tiles made by hand ever being exactly alike. By contrast, machine produced and mechanically decorated tiles had a regulated finish, which resulted in a more guaranteed outcome in terms of the exact size of tiles and the standard quality of their decoration. However, hand-work was still needed to put the finishing touches to tiles, and this was often the task of female workers. Dust-pressed relief tiles needed to have opaque or translucent glazes applied by hand, while transfer prints were stuck to the tiles by hand and once transferred, often coloured in by hand before glazing.

The lot of tile makers and decorators was not always an easy one. Spending long hours each day at one and the same task, such as dust pressing tiles, applying glazes or tinting transfer

Tile with a printed photographic reproduction entitled 'Queen's Apartments, Tutbury '99', executed on a dust-pressed blank by the Photo Decorated Tile Company in 1899.

prints must have been both hard and monotonous work. Added to this were the health hazards. Inhalation of clay dust could cause potter's asthma, while constant contact with lead-based glazes could result in lead poisoning. William J. Furnival's 852-page compendium on the nineteenth-century tile industry, which was published in 1904 under the title *Leadless Decorative Tiles, Faience, and Mosaic*, opens with the statement that 'The object of writing and publishing the following pages is not simply to issue a dissertation upon the history and manufacture of decorative faience and mosaic ... the principal aim is, to place before those who are either interested in, or engaged in these manufactures throughout the world, a series of recipes for the preparation of leadless glazes for the purpose, and so to assist in eliminating lead-poisoning from the industry.' Furnival's crusade against the use of lead glazes did much to reduce this problem in the ceramics industry.

During the second half of the nineteenth century machine production was condemned on aesthetic as well as moral grounds by, among others, John Ruskin and William Morris. Unfortunately the reintroduction of a craft-based industry, which they espoused, did not prove realistic. Morris discovered that his handmade products, including tiles, were very expensive to make and consequently only available to the wealthy. Nor could large enough quantities be made, even if their price had been lower. The virtue of machine production was quantity at an available price.

The Industrial Revolution affected not only the manufacture but also the market for tiles. During the nineteenth century, towns grew considerably, and more stringent building regulations came into force, which put a new emphasis on hygiene. Machine-made tiles with their bright, easily cleanable surfaces were ideal. In addition, tiles added an important element of form and colour to architecture. In the home they were used in kitchens, bathrooms, toilets, fireplaces, porches and entrance halls. In the case of public, commercial and educational buildings, tiles began to be used on an ever-increasing scale in town halls, hospitals, libraries, railway stations, public conveniences, public houses, schools, banks, warehouses and offices. The developing Victorian leisure industry saw the building of music halls, theatres, seaside hotels, winter gardens and pavilions, in all of which tiles found a use.

The application of machine-made tiles in architecture was actively encouraged by architects and designers. For example, in *Hints on*

Detail of the bathroom wall, with Mintons China Works relief tiles, and picture tiles designed by William Wise.

Moulded and glazed plaque of a classical female figure, made by Burmantofts in Leeds *circa* 1890.

Tiles were used both inside and outside public houses to great effect. Bright, shiny tiles on the exterior helped the pub stand out among other buildings, while in the interior tiles were used on the walls, floors, and sometimes the front of the bar as well. They were obviously hygienic, but they could also help create an atmosphere of gaiety and splendour. Late nineteenth- and early twentieth-century pubs in particular have interiors that are rich with decorative glazed tiles, glass mirrors, polished brass and shiny mahogany.

LEFT
Interior of the basement bar at the Royal York Hotel, York. The walls and ceiling are lined with tiles and faience made by Burmantofts, *circa* 1885.

RIGHT
The Crown Liquor Saloon
in Great Victoria Street,
Belfast, opened its doors
about a hundred years ago
and is now owned by the
National Trust. It is still an
active pub, however, with
a carefully preserved
interior which includes its
original gas lighting. Its
splendid tiled facade is
composed of glazed
machine-pressed relief
tiles and architectural
ceramics, all made by
Craven Dunnill. Inside,
there is a tiled floor and
sturdy ceramic bar by the
same manufacturer.

OPPOSITE
The interior of the Crown
Liquor Saloon, Belfast,
with tiles made by Craven
Dunnill, *circa* 1890.

ABOVE
The Royal Dairy at Windsor is part of the Home Farm at Frogmore, and was built in 1858 under the close supervision of Prince Albert. The interior of the creamery has ornately printed wall tiles, and special non-slip tiles on the floor, all supplied by Minton, Hollins & Company. There are glazed faience panels of appropriate figurative scenes, and a glazed frieze running round the top of the walls, with profile heads of the royal children.

RIGHT
The former dairy of *circa* 1885 at The Tower, Penrhos, Anglesey, now converted into a kitchen. The walls are covered with Minton, Hollins & Company printed tiles. The panel over the stove is based on a design by William Wise, while the large panel in the corner was painted by W. P. Simpson. Blue-and-white mosaic tiles cover the floor.

From the turn of the century until the 1930s, Sainsbury's used ceramic tiles extensively in their shops. Their 'Green Dragon' tiles in particular became something of a trademark. Here they can be seen in the frieze at the top of the wall.

Detail of the machine-pressed 'Green Dragon' tiles made for Sainsbury's by Minton, Hollins & Company.

Household Taste, published in 1868 and influential in both Britain and America, Charles Lock Eastlake showed he was an ardent believer in the use of tiles for domestic purposes. When discussing suitable forms of decoration for a hall floor he wrote 'There can be little doubt that the best mode of treating a hall-floor, whether in town or country, is to pave it with encaustic tiles. This branch of art manufacture is one of the most hopeful, in regard to taste, now carried on in this country. It has not only reached great technical perfection as far as material and colour are concerned, but, aided by the designs supplied by many architects of acknowledged skill, it has gradually become a means of decoration which, for beauty of effect, durability, and cheapness, has scarcely a parallel.'

Transfer-printed and relief-pressed glazed tiles became so cheap that builders could afford to install them in all kinds of buildings, even those at the bottom end of the market. There was a particular upsurge in their use for food shops such as butchers and fishmongers. These shops were often tiled from top to bottom with panels depicting cows, sheep, pigs, poultry and fish. Tiled shop interiors have proved very vulnerable to changes in fashion, and relatively few have survived intact to the present day.

The most common application of tiles was their use in cast-iron fireplaces. These were mass produced by firms such as the Carron Ironworks Company in Falkirk, Scotland, or the Coalbrookdale Company in Ironbridge, Shropshire. A choice of tiles was usually available. They were fitted into the frame on a bed of

The availability of mass-produced tiles meant shop interiors could be made more hygienic, particularly food shops such as butchers, fishmongers and greengrocers. The most commonly used tiles in shop interiors were plain white, with decorative friezes or dados of machine-moulded or transfer-printed tiles to add variety. Figurative tile panels could also be included, either inside or out, to indicate the line of business of the shop. They were often hand-painted or slip-trailed, and sometimes included the name of the shop's owner. The illustration (LEFT) shows the interior of a Birmingham butcher's shop, demolished in the 1960s. The walls were covered with ceramic tiles dating from the 1880s, made by Mintons China Works. Both the plain and decorative wall tiles followed a standard layout, which was advertised in Mintons China Works' catalogues as 'Arrangement for Butcher's Shop'. The frieze at the top of the wall shows bulls' heads and swags, while on either side of the cashier there are diagonally placed, transfer-printed tiles designed by William Wise, depicting a bull.

Jack climbs
the Beanstalk.

One of a series of tile panels from the children's ward in the old St Thomas's Hospital, London. Made by Doulton *circa* 1900, and painted by either Margaret Thomson or William Rowe. The ward was closed in the 1970s, but the panels were saved, and have now been restored and are on display in the new hospital. The ward was named after Lilian Holland, whose father donated the panels in her memory.

When railway and underground stations were first built in the nineteenth century, cast iron, glazed bricks and ceramic tiles were soon recognized as the only materials able to sustain the daily wear and tear of thousands of passengers. Tiles are now a common feature of transport architecture, not only because of their abrasion resistant, fire retardant and hygienic qualities, but also because signs, information panels and station names can easily be made from them. Shrubb Hill station, Worcester, is decorated with Maw & Company majolica tiles, dating from 1875 and based on Spanish *cuenca* designs. A section of these is shown in detail below. This is one of the few stations in Britain with Victorian tiles still *in situ*.

The Hull master-builder David Reynard Robinson built 'Farrago' in Hornsea between 1908 and 1909 as his retirement home. His love of tiling led him to cover completely both the inside and outside of the house with English, Dutch and Spanish tiles. However, a careful play of pattern and design was maintained throughout. Here on the landing, encaustic tiles cover the floor, while English and Dutch tiles cover the walls.

A splendid Maw &
Company decorative tile
pavement of *circa* 1870 at
the Bar Convent in York.
It consists of an oblong
central design, made up of
encaustic tiles, surrounded
by plain mosaic tiles.
These combine to make a
simple but effective
repeating pattern.

Page 78 from a Maw &
Company catalogue,
showing the patented
mosaic floor tiles first
introduced in the
mid-1860s which were a
speciality of the firm. Once
the tiles had been laid,
cement was rubbed into
their indentations,
creating a convincing
illusion of a real Roman-
style mosaic.

Neo-Tudor fireplace in the library of Oxburgh Hall, Norfolk, designed in the 1850s by J. C. Buckler. The tiles bear the arms and monogram of the 6th Baronet of Bedingfeld. Their design shows the influence of A.W.N. Pugin, but in origin these tiles go back to late fourteenth-century blue-and-white and lustre floor tiles, of the type used in the palaces of the Dukes of Burgundy.

MAW & C.º BENTHALL WORKS
WORCESTER · 1850 · BENTHALL · 1852 · REBUILT · 1883

MAWS CRAFT CENTRE

ABOVE
The entrance to the Maw & Company factory at Jackfield. Built by Charles Lynam in 1883, at its peak it was one of the biggest tile factories in the world.

RIGHT
Tile panel at Postman's Park, King Edward's Street, London. Part of a series erected in 1900 as a national memorial to brave and selfless deeds by Victorian men and women. The scheme was initiated by the painter G. F. Watts in cooperation with Doulton.

THOMAS GRIFFIN
FITTERS · LABOURER
APRIL · 12 · 1899 · IN A
BOILER EXPLOSION AT A
BATTERSEA SUGAR REFINERY
WAS FATALLY SCALDED IN
RETURNING TO SEARCH
FOR HIS MATE

WALTER · PEART DRIVER
AND HARRY · DEAN FIREMAN
OF THE WINDSOR EXPRESS
ON JULY · 18 · 1898
WHILST BEING SCALDED & BURNT
SACRIFICED THEIR LIVES IN
SAVING THE TRAIN

MARY ROGERS
STEWARDESS OF THE STEL
MAR · 30 · 1899
SELF SACRIFICED BY GIVING
HER LIFE BELT AND VOLUNTA
GOING DOWN IN THE
SINKING SHIP

JOSEPH ANDREW FORD
AGED 30 · METROPOLITAN FIRE
BRIGADE · SAVED SIX PERSONS
FROM FIRE IN GRAYS INN ROAD
BVT IN HIS LAST HEROIC ACT
HE WAS SCORCHED TO DEATH
OCT · 7 · 1871

AMELIA KENNEDY
AGED 19
DIED IN TRYING TO
SAVE HER SISTER
FROM THEIR BVRNING HOVSE
IN EDWARD'S LANE STOKE
NEWINGTON · OCT 18 · 1871

EDMUND EMERY
272 KING'S ROAD CHE
PASSENGER
LEAPT FROM A THAM
STEAMBOAT TO RESCU
CHILD AND WAS DROWN
JULY 31 · 1

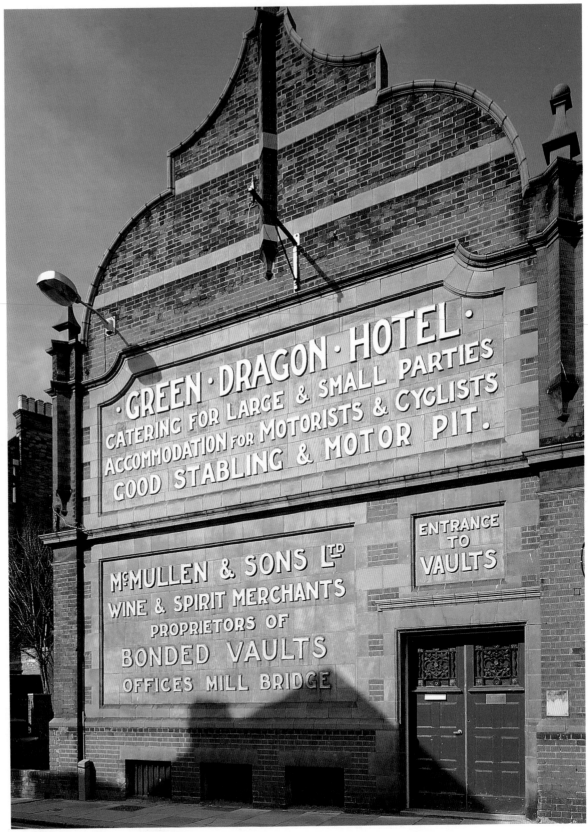

The Gentlemen's Cloakroom in the City Club, London. It has a complete ceramic interior, including the ceiling, made by the Leeds firm of Burmantofts in 1907.

Glazed machine-pressed relief tiles in the King Edward VII urinal at Wolferton Royal railway station, Norfolk, dating from *circa* 1898.

plaster – a row of five or six tiles on either side of the grate provided a safe, fireproof surface, and aided the reflection of heat back into the room. They also provided an element of colour and decoration in the domestic interior, and by the end of the nineteenth century almost every home had a tiled grate.

In this expanding economy, new firms were established. Distribution was facilitated by an extensive canal and railway network, and tiles could now be transported to any part of the country. Until 1850, Minton had enjoyed a virtual monopoly on the manufacture and sale of tiles, but during the second half of the nineteenth century, many rival firms came into being. In 1850 Maw and Company was founded by George Maw, who had bought the defunct tile-making business of the Worcester

Tiled gatepost of Penkelly House, on the main road between Lugwardine and Withington in Hertfordshire. The house was built in 1875 for William Henry Godwin, whose own Godwin tile factory supplied the circular glazed encaustic tiles of the Four Seasons.

Porcelain Company. Maws stayed in Worcester for two years before moving to Broseley near Ironbridge, where they soon became established as a major producer of encaustic floor and dust-pressed wall tiles. In 1883 they moved into a purpose-built factory at Jackfield near Ironbridge, and became one of the biggest tile producers in Britain. T. & R. Boote at Burslem also began making tiles in the 1850s. They took quick advantage of the market opened up by the new dust-pressed encaustic tiles invented by William Boulton and Joseph Worthington in 1863. This type of tile was now within the reach of ordinary householders. In 1852 the Godwin factory began production in Lugwardine near Hereford, and concentrated specifically on encaustic tiles. The Architectural Pottery Company opened at Poole in 1854, and Craven Dunnill was established in 1871 at Jackfield. Existing pottery firms such as Wedgwood and Doulton also began to produce wall tiles. A

FAR LEFT
The gravestone of James Monk, who died in 1872, in the graveyard of Lugwardine parish church, Hertfordshire. The single glazed encaustic tile was made by the firm of Godwin's at Lugwardine.

string of later Staffordshire tile firms followed, for example W. & E. Corn, Sherwin & Cotton, and Malkin Edge & Company.

Many tile firms were established according to the traditional potbank plan, which usually had an open yard in the centre with bottle kilns and workshops clustered around it. The ever-increasing demand for tiles made it obvious that the potbank layout was not the most efficient for large-scale specialist tile production. A new type of building came into being – the purpose-built tile factory. The first of these was built for Minton, Hollins & Company at Stoke-on-Trent in 1869, followed by Craven Dunnill & Company at Jackfield in 1874 and Maw & Company, also at Jackfield, in 1883. The architect of all three was Charles Lynam. They were designed on the principle of 'linear production'. Raw materials entered at one end and the finished product came out at the other. However, not all was merely functional. The frontage of the Minton, Hollins & Company factory, which housed the offices and showrooms, was given a distinguished facade decorated with tiles where it faced a main road. Inside, the walls of the staircase were covered with fine majolica tiles, decorated with Hollins's own monogram. This was clearly meant to demonstrate the power and prestige of the factory owner and to impress visitors. The needs of the workers were also taken into account: there were spacious working conditions and the factory was well ventilated. There was also heating in most parts of the factory, and steam power was used to drive heavy machinery.

GERMANY, FRANCE AND BELGIUM

The developments in the machine production of tiles pioneered in Britain were soon followed in other European countries, notably Germany, France and Belgium. In Germany the most important nineteenth-century firm was Villeroy & Boch, who had factories in Dresden, at Mettlach near the border with Luxemburg, and at Septfontaines in Luxemburg. The English inventions and manufacturing techniques were soon adopted at the latter in particular. After a visit to some Staffordshire factories in 1823, J. F. Boch set up a transfer-printing workshop at Septfontaines. R. E. Forrer, in his *Geschichte der europäischen Fliesenkeramik* of 1901, mentions the introduction of dust pressing at Septfontaines as early as 1846.

During the second half of the nineteenth century and the beginning of the twentieth, most of Villeroy & Boch's tile production was carried out at Mettlach and Dresden. Mettlach was the most important of the two, with the Dresden factory producing only a small number of wall, stove and mosaic tiles. In 1869 a separate factory was set up at Mettlach for floor and wall tile production, and plain floor and encaustic tiles were produced in great quantities. The encaustic tiles became known throughout Europe as 'Mettlacher Platten', and were used extensively in churches and public buildings. Prestige commissions also came from abroad, including the large tile panels on the exterior walls of the Rijksmuseum in Amsterdam, which were supplied by Villeroy & Boch in 1883. The increasing freedom of worship enjoyed by Catholics in Holland during the nineteenth century tied in with the neo-Gothic revival in architecture, and many new Roman Catholic churches were built, whose architects, in the absence of Dutch encaustic tiles, turned

OPPOSITE
One of a series of panels on the exterior of the Rijksmuseum, Amsterdam, made by Villeroy & Boch in 1883. The series celebrates famous artists and events in the history of Dutch art. The sculptors Claus Sluter and Jan Aertsz. Terwen are depicted here, together with the architect Hendrik de Keyser.

Ecclesiastical floor tiles of 1881, made by Villeroy & Boch for the Roman Catholic neo-Gothic Sint Nicolaaskerk at Ijsselstein, near Utrecht.

to Germany for supplies. The neo-Gothic church in Ijsselstein, Holland, has a superb floor of Villeroy & Boch encaustics *in situ*. Orders for the firm came from as far afield as Russia, where their tiles were laid in the Bolshoi Theatre in Moscow.

Dust-pressed wall tiles were decorated in a variety of ways. If transfer printing and machine relief pressing were the main techniques, hand painting was still used for important one-off commissions. The Pfund Dairy in Dresden is good example. Paul and Friedrich Pfund ran a successful business in dairy products and ordered an elaborate hand-painted scheme for their shop from Villeroy & Boch in 1892. It survived the terrible firebombing of

Dresden in 1945, and still exists today. Mass production techniques were, however, necessary to meet the great demand for Art Nouveau tiles at the turn of the century. Villeroy & Boch opened a new factory to cater for this market at Dänischburg near Lübeck in 1906.

Rival German tile manufacturers came into being from the 1860s onwards. The Norddeutsche Steingutfabrik in Grohn, near Bremen, was founded in 1869, and was followed in 1877 by Servais & Cie in Ehrang, near Trier, and by Georg Bankel, who set up a factory in Laufan-der-Pegnitz, near Nürnberg, in 1889. Wessel's Wandplatten Fabrik began production in Bonn in 1896. Until the First World War, Germany experienced a boom in the production of

VILLEROY & BOCH

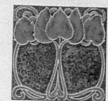

827b*

793b*

740*

827*

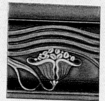

868a*

668*

733*

869*

868b*

801*

a   674*   b

874*

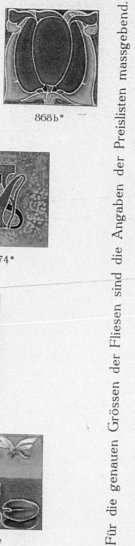

a   b   737*   c   d

a   b   c 731*   d   e

a   b   c 732*   d   e

Für die genauen Grössen der Fliesen sind die Angaben der Preislisten massgebend.

Page from a Villeroy & Boch catalogue of *circa* 1910. It shows a range of machine-pressed tiles decorated with transfer-printed designs or relief patterns, painted with coloured glazes. The curvilinear form of German *Jugendstil*, as well as a more geometric, abstract variety, can be seen in the design of the tiles.

dust-pressed Art Nouveau wall tiles, for which there was also a lucrative export market.

Developments in Germany were in some ways echoed in France, as tile manufacturers quickly became aware of the advantages of new technology, and incorporated dust pressing, machine-moulded decoration and transfer printing into their production methods. In Paris, the firm of Loebnitz et Fils was one of the most successful. In 1834 they were established under the name of Pichenot, and specialized in stove tiles which won prizes in various exhibitions, but in 1855 the firm came under the direction of Jules Loebnitz. When facades decorated with tiles and architectural ceramics became fashionable towards the end of the century, Loebnitz were ready to furnish archi-

tects with a complete range of products. They also made their mark at international exhibitions, where they supplied tiles and faience for various exhibition pavilions. The entrance of the Palais des Beaux-Arts at the 1889 Paris Exhibition was an example of their work. French tile firms operated very much within their own geographical locations, and Loebnitz tiles are therefore most common in the Paris area.

Beauvais and its surrounding regions were home to many tile manufacturers. The vogue for decorating facades with tiles and multi-coloured ceramics was originally inspired by Parisian examples, but the Beauvais architects developed their own unique style, in cooperation with the local tile producers. Firms such as Gréber matched Loebnitz step-for-step in

The facade of the Charles Gréber tile and terracotta factory at 63 rue de Calais, Beauvais, built in 1911. Terracotta lizards (shown in detail above) scale the tiled wall, and the central feature of the facade shows a potter at his wheel.

The nineteenth-century Boulenger tile factory has left an extraordinary legacy in the small town of Auneuil, south-west of Beauvais. Decorative inlaid tiles were used to cover the floors and facades of several buildings, including the factory itself, the large vestibule of the church, the café-hotel and the local museum, which is dedicated to Boulenger tiles. Although the factory has ceased to operate, lack of development in the area has fortunately left all these buildings standing. The people of Auneuil are aware of the importance of their tiled buildings, and a restoration programme is under way to ensure they continue to survive as permanent features of the town.

terms of range and quality of products. Encaustic tiles were also manufactured in Beauvais itself. Colozier had a large factory at Saint-Just-des-Marais, on the outskirts of the town.

The most interesting manufacturer of encaustic tiles in the region was Boulenger, who operated in the small town of Auneuil, some eleven kilometres south-west of Beauvais. The works used to dominate the town, and even today much evidence still survives around Auneuil from this great period of French tile production. The Boulenger factory, which was built in 1883, can still be seen today, and has many fine encaustic tiles on its facade and side walls. The local church has a vestibule with an elaborate tiled dado supplied by Boulenger, but the most extraordinary building is the Boulenger museum, built in 1885 to house a collection of the firm's best products. The whole building is covered from top to bottom with encaustic tiles of every description, while many unique examples of Boulenger tiles are displayed inside. Boulenger's most prestigious commission was to make tiles for the mortuary chapel of Napoleon III at St Mary's Church, Chislehurst, Kent. (Napoleon III had fled to

England after the Franco-Prussian War of 1870–71.) Special tiles were made bearing the N of Napoleon and the Napoleonic eagle.

Other large tile producers were active at Paray-le-Monial, Saône et Loire, where the Société Anonyme des Carrelages Céramique made encaustic tiles, and in and near Maubeuge near the French-Belgian border. From there the firms of Douzies and Boch Frères supplied the northern parts of France with their products. The Boch Frères factory at Maubeuge was a French branch of the massive Belgian Boch Frères factory at La Louvière, in southern Belgium. Boch Frères at La Louvière had a diverse production consisting of sanitary ware and various forms of wall and floor tiles.

RIGHT
Detail of the tiled vestibule of Auneuil parish church, built *circa* 1875. The central tile depicts the Agnus Dei.

ABOVE RIGHT
The Boulenger family tomb in the graveyard at Cauvigny, Oise. Encaustic tiles cover both its interior and exterior. The monument is somewhat neglected and in need of restoration.

HOLLAND, SPAIN AND PORTUGAL

The three European countries where tin-glazed tile production had always been strongest were Holland, Spain and Portugal. Although the changes brought about by machine production caused a sharp decline in the export market for Dutch tin-glazed tiles, several firms continued to make them as demand never entirely disappeared. Towards the end of the nineteenth century, new firms were established who embraced the technology of dust-pressed tiles; for example Rozenburg in The Hague, and De Distel in Amsterdam. Some well-established firms, such as De Porceleyne Fles in Delft, who had been making tin-glazed wares since the seventeenth century, introduced dust pressing alongside traditional production techniques. For the most part, even Dutch machine-made tiles were painted by hand or decorated by the stencil method, where ceramic pigment is brushed through thin sheets of metal with cut-out designs. It can therefore be argued that the craft process of hand decorating persisted much longer in Holland than in neighbouring countries.

Hand-decorated, dust-pressed tiles can still be seen in many places, including the railway stations at Haarlem and Leeuwarden, which have tiles supplied by Rozenburg. In Amsterdam many porches of houses built at the turn of the century feature dust-pressed tiles with stencil decorations, made by De Porceleyne Fles. De Distel made hand-painted, dust-pressed tiles with elaborate figurative scenes which were used in shops and the entrances to large houses. The firms of Regout and Société

Tiled porches and house entrances became fashionable from the mid-nineteenth century onwards. The tiles were usually employed on the walls of the porch, sometimes in combination with special floor tiles. Both fulfilled a functional as well as a decorative role. The machine-pressed glazed wall tiles and hard-wearing floor quarries could easily be washed and helped to keep the entrance clean. There was also scope for enhancing the appearance of the house, ranging from simple tiles with decorative insets for modest dwellings, to large, elaborately painted compositions for the homes of the well-to-do. This hand-painted tile panel, *circa* 1910, of a winter scene, is set in a porch on the Koninginneweg, Hilversum. The panel is signed with the initials UTHW, which probably stand for Utrechtse Tegel Handel Westraven.

ABOVE
Name panel of hand-painted tiles, *circa* 1910, above the entrance of a house on Prinses Clementinalaan, Ghent.

BELOW LEFT
Tiles are mainly applied to the facades of houses as a form of decoration. They are often used to accentuate windows and doorways, or appear as friezes under the eaves. Sometimes tiled panels with the name of the house can be seen, usually placed above the main entrance. The decorations range from simple machine-pressed designs and transfer-printed patterns to elaborately painted figurative schemes. In this way tiles once served as an index to the wealth and status of the householder; but mass production eventually made it possible for tiles to be used on the facades of even the smallest homes. These transfer-printed tiles are on the facade of a house at Gistelse Steenweg 78, Bruges.

RIGHT
Hand-painted blue-and-white frieze of 1887 above the factory shop of De Porceleyne Fles on the market square in Delft. The frieze, depicting various stages in pottery making, was designed by Le Comte and painted by Leon Senf, whose signature can be seen in the bottom left corner.

Céramique, both at Maastricht, made dust-pressed tiles with transfer-printed decorations.

Alfred Regout's factory was mainly concerned with the production of tableware with transfer-printed decorations. He is known to have imported engraved copperplates from England, which may explain why the technique of transfer printing on tiles became so readily established here towards the end of the nineteenth century. Moreover, the physical location of Maastricht puts it in very close proximity to Belgium and Germany, where similar production techniques were commonplace. Regout was so taken by all things English that his tile trademark was an *R* within a diamond shape, echoing the English diamond-shaped registration marks in use until 1883. His tiles were even sold in Britain, where they were used in fireplaces.

Tin-glazed tile production in Spain remained strong well into the twentieth century. The demand for tiles had always been high in that country, particularly in Catalonia, Valencia and

Detail of a wall decorated
with tiles and a ceramic
flower of *circa* 1900 on the
rue Victor Hugo, Beauvais.

Andalusia, but even here machine production made inroads into the strongly established tradition of handmade and hand-painted tiles. Floor tiles were machine-made by Miguel Nolla in Valencia and by the firm of Escofet, Tejara y Cia in Barcelona, and machine-pressed *cuenca* tiles became a large-scale industry in Seville, where Pickman, Ramos Rejano and Mensaque Rodriguez specialized in them. Their *cuenca* tiles often show Moorish designs, whose origins go back to the fourteenth century.

In Portugal hand-painted tiles remained an established part of nineteenth- and twentieth-century tile production, but stencilling was introduced in order to increase output, particularly for the very large areas of tiling used to cover facades. Dust pressing was introduced by the Sacavém factory in Lisbon during the late nineteenth century for transfer-printed or machine-moulded tiles with relief decorations. These machine-made tiles look very indifferent and out of place among the many examples of handmade tiles, but hand-painted or stencilled tin-glazed tiles often have simple designs that work well when repeated on a large scale. Detailed transfer-printed designs become rather meaningless when used in this way. This is in contrast to Spain, where *cuenca* tiles lent themselves much better to machine production, perhaps because the original technique had been simply to mould the plastic clay with a stamp. The machine intervention in this case resulted in a more uniform product, but one that remained visually acceptable.

The first hurdle in the story of mechanized tile production had been to find solutions to the technical problems of making and decorating them. Once this had been solved, matters of good design had to be considered. The mass production of tiles affected architects and

APPLICATION DE NOS PRODUITS
à l'installation d'une salle de bains
REVÊTEMENTS, CARRELAGES, TOILETTE ET APPAREILS

designers in different ways. Some tried to work positively with it, while others reacted sharply against it and turned back to craft techniques. Whichever side an architect or designer was on, machine production generated debate about the importance of design, and one positive result was the emergence of individual designers of note.

4

THE TRIUMPH OF
THE DESIGNER

The adoption of the principles of mass production created the problem of how art might be reconciled to industry. During the early part of the Industrial Revolution, the designers of tiles often remained in obscurity within the production system, and we know little of the individuals concerned. But in the second half of the nineteenth century, tile manufacturers began to use prominent designers, either 'in-house' or on a freelance basis, with the conscious aim of improving the appearance of their tiles. These designers not only emerged as named individuals from the vast mass production system, they also showed that good creative design was possible within the constraints of mechanical processes. At the

Casa Batlló in Barcelona, built between 1904 and 1906. Gaudí made the ridged roof, shown here in detail, look like the back of a dragon, while broken mosaic tiles create bizarre effects on the turret and chimney stack.

Detail of a bench in Park Güell. The butterfly tile was first shattered, then carefully reassembled.

same time, there were other designers who turned their backs on the Industrial Revolution and set about reviving the production of hand-made and hand-decorated tiles which they held to be superior to mass-produced examples. In a further development, several outstanding architects in Britain and on the Continent began to use tiles as a creative part of architectural design.

TILE DESIGNERS

The influence of the machine on the quality of design was a much-debated issue throughout the nineteenth century. As early as 1840, in an article entitled 'The Fine Arts in Florence', published in the *Quarterly Review*, the antiquarian and fellow of the Royal Society Sir Francis Palgrave (1788–1861) castigated machine design as 'perpetually branded by mediocrity'. The Great Exhibition of 1851 demonstrated the wonders of machine production, but it also brought about an increased awareness of the limitations inherent in mechanical decoration techniques. To some the cheapness of machine production was matched by the nastiness of its design.

The opposing viewpoints were summed up succinctly by the artist and critic Lewis F. Day in his article 'Machine Made Art', published in the *Art Journal* of 1885.

There are two opinions upon the subject of machine made Art. The more modern, that is to say, the more scientific, school of thinkers, are disposed to look upon machinery as the key to everything that is hopeful in the future. Artists, on the other hand, are apt to complain that it is a veritable Juggernaut, under whose wheels the arts must eventually be crushed out of existence.

Machine-pressed tiles decorated with stamped relief designs and transfer prints were responsible for much mediocre design. The enormous range of tile patterns produced during the nineteenth century included many that were tawdry in appearance, particularly the indifferently printed tiles with repetitive designs that were used in houses at the bottom end of the market. Floor tiles frequently copied medieval designs, while designs for wall tiles were often cribbed from historical patterns found in the various grammars of ornament in circulation at that time. The designer W. P. Simpson, for example, designed sets of transfer-printed tiles for Minton, Hollins & Company in the early 1870s, and at least eighteen of his designs were lifted straight from *Microcosm*, W. H. Pyne's book of illustrations, which had first been published in 1808. All this, it could be argued, did not say much for the imagination of the designer.

To solve the problem of the piracy of designs, Britain had strengthened the Copyright of Design Act in 1842 by creating more classes of protected ornamental designs. Ceramics was one of these, and tile designs were also registered, but piracy continued nonetheless. Many designs were never registered, and therefore not protected by the Act, while those that were registered were only protected for a limited period. From the point of view of the historian, it is unfortunate that tile designs were registered in the name of their manufacturer, rather than their designer, which would have provided a far more useful historical record.

The role of the tile designer became more prominent as the nineteenth century wore on. Early tile manufacturers, such as Minton, Chamberlain and Copeland had concentrated on technical improvements in manufacturing

Collection of late
nineteenth-century tiles
by William De Morgan,
Mintons China Works,
W. B. Simpson & Sons and
Wedgwood.

RIGHT
Pencil design by William
Wise, *circa* 1878, for a tile
in the series 'Rustic
Scenes'.

FAR RIGHT
Transfer-printed tile made
by Mintons China Works
from William Wise's
design.

methods and decoration techniques, such as encaustic tile making, underglaze transfer printing, lithographic printing, and majolica glazes. But by the time of the Great Exhibition of 1851, many of these technical problems had been solved, and more attention could be given to matters of design.

Encaustic floor tiles dominated the early tile market, and were often designed by architects. A.W.N.Pugin was associated with Minton, L.N.Cottingham and H.Eginton with Chamberlain, and J. P. Seddon with Maw. The design of wall tiles attracted a wider range of artists. Some designers produced mediocre products by relying on copying and repeating the designs of others, but several creative designers of note emerged during the second half of the nineteenth century.

In Britain, Owen Jones, Walter Crane, William Wise, John Moyr Smith, William Morris, William De Morgan, C. F. A. Voysey, Sir Edward John Poynter and William J. Neatby were some of the many designers who worked

on tiles. On the Continent, Jacobus van den Bosch and Adolf Le Comte in Holland, and Max Laeuger in Germany were tile designers of distinction. Their attitudes toward mechanical tile production varied greatly. Some embraced the new inventions, while others placed higher value on craft methods of production.

In his *Designs for Mosaic and Tessellated Pavements* (1842), Owen Jones welcomed the invention of dust pressing and the possibilities it opened up for mosaic tile manufacture. He opens his account with the words: 'The object of the following pages is to call public attention to a new material for Tessellated Pavements, and to an improved method of constructing the same, by the adoption of which this ancient and esteemed mode of decoration may be re-introduced, at a moderate cost, for the embellishment of our modern buildings.'

Many tile manufacturers had a range of artists working for them who happily cooperated with mechanical means of decoration, particularly various forms of printing. John

Moyr Smith produced many picture tile series for Mintons China Works and Minton, Hollins & Company, and these demonstrate that in his designs he took into account both the constraints and advantages inherent in block printing. He exploited it with great success, and his tiles are a good example of what can be done if a designer works with certain printing methods in mind and cooperates positively with their requirements.

Transfer printing from engraved or etched copperplates allowed for fine line work and the depiction of detailed scenes. This method was used by Walter Crane, who created picture tile series for Maw & Company, and William Wise, who worked for Mintons China Works. The subject matter they depicted varied greatly. Crane designed tiles showing nursery rhymes and mythological subjects, while Wise created farmyard scenes and landscapes of great charm. Their printed designs were often coloured by hand, thereby successfully combining two apparently opposing methods of decoration. Their tiles were used in fireplaces, on walls and in certain types of furniture.

Some excellent designs for machine-pressed tiles were made by the architect and designer C. F. A. Voysey. Although normally associated with the Arts and Crafts movement, Voysey was not so dogmatic as to fail to recognize the potential, in the right circumstances, of machine production. At the turn of the century, he designed some very fine tiles for Pilkingtons, in which he reduced complex natural forms to well-designed flat shapes and lines suitable for dust-pressed line relief tiles.

Sir Edward John Poynter was a major figure in the late Victorian art establishment, both in his capacity as Director of the National Gallery, and as President of the Royal Academy. As an artist his work was firmly set within the classical academic tradition. This can clearly be seen in the designs he executed for the former Grill Room of the Victoria & Albert Museum.

The Dutch designer Adolf Le Comte worked for the well-established Delft firm of De Porceleyne Fles, which began to make dust-pressed tiles towards the end of the nineteenth century. Many of these were decorated with the aid of stencils, for which Le Comte designed strikingly simple Art Nouveau motifs, based on plants and flowers.

The strongest reaction against machine-made goods came from the Arts and Crafts movement. Many of the ideas of this movement about the nature and value of handmade

Panel of six tiles made by Pilkingtons, with machine-pressed relief decoration of a repeating pattern of fish and waterlilies. Designed by C. F. A. Voysey, *circa* 1903.

PICTURE·TILES·DESIGNED·BY·WALTER·CRANE

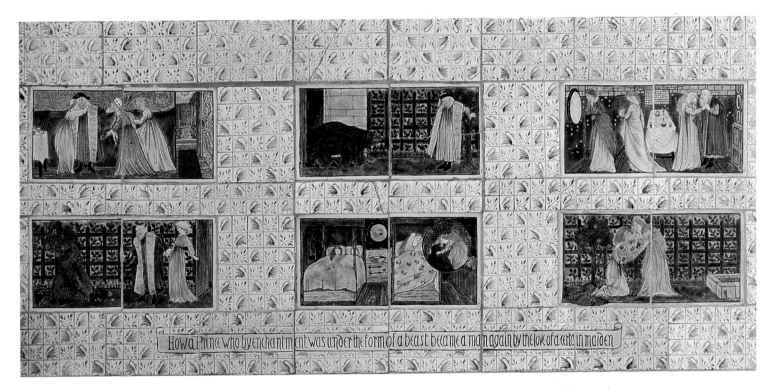

How a Prince who by enchantment was under the form of a beast became a man again by the love of a certe in maiden

goods were inherited from John Ruskin and the views he put forward in *The Stones of Venice*. The basic tenet of Ruskin's argument was that men were debased by the machine. 'It is not that men are ill fed, but that they have no pleasure in the work by which they make their bread and therefore look to wealth as the only means of pleasure.' Frequent comparisons were made with medieval craftsmen who, according to Ruskin, were not enslaved by division of labour and machine production, and who were a part of the whole process of manufacture, from beginning to end. This gave them satisfaction in the goods they made, rather than the wage they earned being their only goal.

William Morris was much influenced by Ruskin's ideas, and put words into deeds when he set up the firm of Morris, Marshall, Faulkner & Company in 1861. Morris & Co., as it is usually known, manufactured handmade furniture, stained glass, wallpaper and textiles, as well as decorated tiles. The firm used designs by Philip Webb, Sir Edward Burne-Jones and Dante Gabriel Rossetti, as well as those by William Morris himself. They bought handmade, white glazed tiles from Holland, decorated them with figurative scenes and patterns painted on the glaze, and fired them in the same kiln used to produce their stained glass. In the 1860s scenes from fairy-tales including Beauty and the Beast, Cinderella and Sleeping Beauty, designed by Burne-Jones, were popular. Tiles decorated with angels, minstrels and the Labours of the Months were also made. The style of painting was clear and direct, and in line with Morris's view of medieval handwork. Tiles with simple repeating patterns of daisies or swans were used as surrounds for the more

ABOVE
Panel of six scenes illustrating the story of Beauty and the Beast, designed by Sir Edward Burne-Jones in 1864. The scenes were painted in the workshop of Morris, Marshall, Faulkner & Company in London, on blank tiles imported from Holland.

OPPOSITE
Plate no. 59 from a Maw & Company catalogue of *circa* 1880, with a series of subjects designed by Walter Crane. They show characters from nursery rhymes and the four elements.

Tile made in William Morris's workshop, *circa* 1865. The decoration has been painted on-glaze, on to a white glazed Dutch blank. The floral motif corresponds exactly to one of the elements in the design of Morris's 1861 'Daisy' wallpaper.

Swan pattern tile made by Morris & Co., *circa* 1865. The design is attributed to Philip Webb, and has been painted with blue on-glaze enamel on a Dutch handmade tin-glazed tile.

figurative examples. The tiles themselves were used in fireplaces and overmantels, and therefore formed part of the firm's wide range of products for interior decoration.

Judging by his own textile, wallpaper and tile designs, Morris was concerned that his floral and foliage motifs should be in harmony with the flat surfaces to which they were applied, and simplified his complex natural forms accordingly. He shunned excessive naturalism in design, as he made clear in one of his lectures, entitled 'Some Hints on Pattern Designing', and first delivered at the Working Men's College, London, on 10 December 1881.

In pottery-painting we are more than ever in danger of falling into sham naturalistic platitude, since we have no longer to stamp our designs with a rough wood-block on paper or cotton, nor have we to build up our outlines by laying square by square of colour, but pencil [brush] in hand, may do pretty much what we will. So we must be a law to

ourselves, and when we get a tile or a plate to ornament remember two things: first, the confined space or odd shape we have to work in; & second, the way in which the design has to be executed.

However, this concern with design was not always matched by a proper knowledge of ceramic techniques. Technically, Morris & Co. tile decoration left much to be desired. A lack of understanding of ceramic pigments and on-glaze decorative techniques led to the deterioration of many of their tiles. This is perhaps the reason why production of Morris & Co. tiles was franchised to the Dutch tile factory of Ravesteyn in the 1880s. Not only did the Dutch make and decorate tiles in a way which came close to Morris's own ideas about handwork, but Dutch tin-glazed tiles were painted in-glaze, which is much more durable than the on-glaze technique employed at Morris & Co. Well-known Morris tile patterns such as 'daisy', 'bough', 'sunflower', 'swan' and 'scroll' were all made in Holland to be used in houses decorated by Morris & Co. These Morris designs can still be seen in Ravesteyn's pattern books of the 1880s. Dutch 'Morris' tiles have stood the test of time much better than Morris's own.

Morris and his close associates frequently used Dutch-made tiles in their own homes as well. For example, they can still be seen at the Red House, Bexley Heath, at Kelmscott House, London, and in the marvellous fireplace with blue-and-white tiles featuring many Morris & Co. designs at Kelmscott Manor, Oxfordshire. A watercolour by Henry Treffry Dunn, dated 1882 and now in the National Portrait Gallery, London, shows Rossetti in his sitting room at Chelsea, next to an open fireplace which is clad on either side with traditional delft tiles.

Fireplace in the Hall of Queens' College, Cambridge. The decorations were hand painted on Dutch tin-glazed tiles in the workshop of Morris, Marshall, Faulkner & Company between 1862 and 1864. Their design and execution represents a truly cooperative effort between William Morris, Burne-Jones, Ford Madox Brown and Rossetti. They show Margaret of Anjou and Elizabeth of Woodville, the angels of day and night, St Bernard and St Margaret, and the Labours of the Months. Swan tiles attributed to Philip Webb fill the spaces between the figurative scenes.

William De Morgan was a close friend of William Morris. They had first met around 1862, when De Morgan became associated with 'the Firm'. De Morgan designed some stained glass and tiles for Morris & Co, but by 1869 was experimenting with the manufacture of his own tiles at his house in Fitzroy Square in London. After an accident, which caused a serious fire, De Morgan was compelled to move to another site, settling at 30, Cheyne Row, Chelsea. His early experiments with lustre painting were done on Dutch tin-glazed blanks, and on other glazed blanks from English firms such as Wedgwood and Carter & Company. Obviously, De Morgan was less averse to using machine-pressed blanks than Morris.

At Chelsea, De Morgan quickly established himself as an independent tile producer. His success meant that he soon needed bigger premises, and in 1882 he moved his tile-making operation to Merton Abbey, Surrey, where he remained until 1888. He then moved again to set up a pottery at Sands End, Fulham, where he went into partnership with the architect Halsey Ricardo. In 1898 the pottery went into liquidation and the partnership with Ricardo was dissolved. A new partnership was formed with three employees – Frank Iles and the brothers Charles and Fred Passenger, which lasted until 1907.

De Morgan was a prolific designer, whose range of designs covered animal, bird and floral motifs, as well as medieval-style sailing boats. His treatment of these in particular reveals his interest in the medieval period, which he shared with Morris. His animal designs, many of which were executed in ruby lustre, are bold and strong, often with a touch of humour. Rabbits, deer, snakes, horses, fishes, eagles, dodos, storks and peacocks are presented with great imagination, and enjoyed a wide popular appeal. His floral designs show his close study of Islamic tiles and pottery, and were painted in brilliant colours such as turquoise, blue, purple, yellow and green.

De Morgan began to make his own tiles from plastic clay during the Chelsea period. These were biscuit fired and coated with white slip. The design was put on to the slip, covered with a clear glaze, and fired for a second time. De Morgan devised a special method to ensure close adherence to the master design. The tile painter would stick the master onto one side of a sheet of glass, the other side of which was covered by a thin piece of paper. The piece of glass was then held up against the light, so that the master design was visible through it, and the painter would carefully trace the original on to the paper. The paper was then placed face down on the slip-coated tile, and the back

OPPOSITE
Panel of William De Morgan tiles, with an Islamic-inspired motif in the centre and Barnard, Bishop & Barnard tiles at top and bottom. Fulham period, 1888–97.

William De Morgan red lustre animal and foliage tiles of 1904–7, in one of the bathrooms at Debenham House, Addison Road, London.

The Arab Hall at Leighton
House, constructed
between 1877 and 1879.
The walls are lined with
authentic sixteenth- and
seventeenth-century
Islamic Iznik tiles, painted
in an underglaze
technique.

ABOVE
Detail of a fireplace at Spring Bank, Headingley, Leeds. De Morgan tiles of *circa* 1880, with a design of yellow sunflowers among green foliage.

LEFT
De Morgan's sense of two-dimensional, strong, intricate design can be seen in this panel of six tiles with Persian decoration, made *circa* 1890.

RIGHT
View of the Grill Room in the Victoria & Albert Museum, London, showing the large panels of the months and the Four Seasons designed by Sir Edward John Poynter between 1868 and 1870. The designs were later executed by the female students of the Minton Art Pottery Studio at Kensington Gore in London.

covered with a clear glaze. The paper disappeared in the firing, and the painting and clear glaze fused with the white slip on to the tile body.

De Morgan's tiles were used on walls and in fireplaces, but also, unusually, in passenger boats of the P & O Line. However, their price meant they could only be afforded by a wealthy clientele. For example, De Morgan made plain, hand-painted, turquoise-coloured tiles for the anteroom and staircase of Leighton House, Holland Park, home of the famous Victorian artist Lord Frederick Leighton, between 1879 and 1881. The remarkable Arab Hall, lined with authentic sixteenth- and seventeenth-century Iznik tiles brought home from the Middle East by Lord Leighton, had just been installed, and the atmosphere thus created of the world of the Arabian Nights must have had a remarkable effect on De Morgan, as many of his tile designs show the influence of Islamic ceramics. Another fine example of the use of De Morgan's tiles is at Debenham House in nearby Addison Road, where they cover both walls and fireplaces.

The opulent use of polychrome ceramics was also practised with great success by others, among them the designer William J. Neatby, who created some fine tiled murals around the turn of the century. In his article 'Mr. W. J. Neatby and his work', published in *The Studio* in 1903, Aymer Vallance stated that it was 'the strength of Mr. Neatby's work, that he is no mere theorist, but at once a designer, vivid in imagination and a handicraftsman who has thoroughly mastered the ways and means of his material.' Neatby had spent some years at the faience and tile manufacturer Burmantofts in Leeds, where he learned about the ceramics trade, before joining Doulton & Company in London in 1890. He was head of the architectural department until 1907, and produced some of his best and most original work during this period, particularly designs for hand-painted panels. These include twenty-eight panels designed for the Winter Gardens, Blackpool, in 1896. They show women dressed in swirling outfits that are equally influenced by pre-Raphaelite designs and by the themes of Art Nouveau. These were followed by a series of extraordinary designs for the polychrome tiles on the exterior of the Everard Building in Bristol in 1901. These colourful Art Nouveau images celebrate the printer's craft by showing Gutenburg and Morris at their hand-operated printing presses. Neatby also designed the tiles for the glorious Harrods Meat Hall in 1902, which, with their hunting and farmyard scenes make up one the best Art Nouveau interior tiling schemes in Britain. It not only provides vibrant colour in the store's interior but also satisfies the need for hygiene.

The British Arts and Crafts movement affected several Continental tile designers, among them the Dutchman Jacobus van den Bosch, who was greatly influenced by C. F. A. Voysey. He adapted Voysey's 'Bird and Tulip' wallpaper, which had been illustrated in *The Studio* of 1896, to create a successful tile pattern. From 1898 to 1900 van den Bosch worked for the Dutch tile firm 'Holland' in Utrecht, where he created a series of Art Nouveau designs for tin-glazed wall tiles for the domestic market, which were published in the form of printed catalogues. They could be used and adapted by architects to suit their needs. Despite being hand-painted, the tiles were made in sufficient quantities to be within the reach of the ordinary householder. The Dutch tin-glazed tile industry had long experience of competitive,

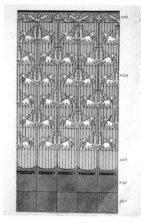

Page from a catalogue issued *circa* 1900 by the firm of 'Holland' in Utrecht, showing a design entitled 'Waterkip' (Water hen) by Jacobus van den Bosch. It is based on a wallpaper pattern by C. F. A. Voysey, illustrated in *The Studio* magazine of 1896, under the title 'Bird and Tulip'.

Tin-glazed tiles in the porch of a house at Koninginneweg 203, Amsterdam, with a hand-painted design by Jacobus van den Bosch. Made by 'Holland' of Utrecht, *circa* 1900.

hence cost-effective tile production. Many of van den Bosch's tile schemes can still be seen in the suburbs of Amsterdam, where they provide a dash of much-needed colour among the drab brown brick facades of turn-of-the-century housing.

In contrast to van den Bosch, whose tiles found a wide and popular appeal, the German designer Max Laeuger, who had also embraced the Arts and Crafts ideal of handwork, specialized in more exclusive commissions. Laeuger was a versatile artist and designer who was artistic director at the Thonwerke ceramics factory at Kandern, Baden, in the Black Forest. In 1908 he was asked by the Swedish architect Anders Lundberg to design and manufacture interior and exterior tiles for a country house which Lundberg was building at Aerdenhout near Bloemendaal on the Dutch coast. Lundberg had received this commission from the wealthy merchant Julius Carl Bunge, who was a Wagner fanatic and wanted 'Kareol', as his

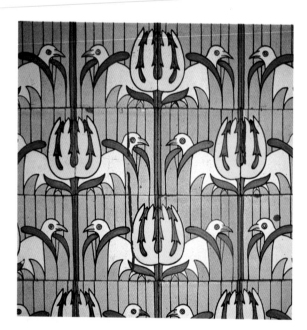

house (now destroyed) was called, to reflect in its design, decoration and setting Wagner's opera *Tristan und Isolde*.

Laeuger made use of over 200 individual tile designs at Kareol. The tiles were set around the house's doors and windows, and were mostly decorated with severe abstract forms, based on floral and foliage motifs, reminiscent of the Viennese Secession designs of the Austrian architects Joseph Olbrich and Josef Hoffmann. Whole panels of figurative tiling were also used, some of which referred directly to the opera — for example that above the entrance to the house, which depicted a Norse sailing ship. The tiles were made of red earthenware, with the designs being first slip-trailed by hand in black, then filled in with various colours including green, ochre, blue, turquoise, white and gold. On the outside of the house, green tiles predominated, in order to blend in with its rural setting.

ARCHITECTS AND TILES

Around the turn of the century, architectural designers came to influence not only the production of tiles, but also their use. William Burges, Norman Shaw and Halsey Ricardo in Britain, Gaudí in Spain, Hendrikus Petrus Berlage and Willem Kromhout in Holland, Hector Guimard and Auguste Perret in France, and Otto Wagner in Vienna began to make innovative use of tiles in architecture, both mass-produced and hand-decorated. They all had in common an ability to integrate tiles in some special way for decorative and functional purposes in their buildings.

William Burges was one of the most original English Gothic Revival architects. His love of medieval-style colour and ornament can be seen in much of his furniture and architectural

Peacock panel from the Wagnerian villa 'Kareol', designed by Max Laeuger in 1908.

design. One of his foremost architectural projects was the restoration of Cardiff Castle for the 3rd Marquess of Bute between 1865 and 1875. Extensive use of figurative and decorative tiles was made throughout the building, on floors, walls and fireplaces.

Norman Shaw built a remarkably fine range of houses in which handmade tiles were a frequent feature. In the early 1870s Shaw would sometimes use Maw & Company tiles. Later he favoured hand-decorated De Morgan tiles. Shaw's association with the Arts and Crafts movement also led him to employ the firm of Morris & Co. The interiors of Swan House in Chelsea, built in 1876, had Morris & Co. tiles as a distinctive feature of the fireplaces. Shaw's gabled Tabbard Inn, built in 1880 in Bath Road,

Bedford Park, London, is still graced with fine De Morgan tiles on the walls in the bar. Shaw also used traditional Dutch tiles: in 1875 in Sutton Place, Surrey. In one of the surviving sketches for the drawing room fireplace of the house, Shaw specifically annotated the words 'Dutch tiles' for either side of the grate.

Halsey Ricardo was an ardent advocate of the use of tiles in architecture. His close friendship and business association with De Morgan put him in a position to use hand-decorated tiles on a large scale. His major architectural creation is Debenham House in Addison Road, London, built for Sir Ernest Debenham between 1904 and 1907. De Morgan tiles with lustre decorations and painted animal designs are found throughout the house in the bathrooms and

LEFT
The Summer Smoking Room at Cardiff
Castle, tiled between 1872 and 1874. It has a
circular floor of encaustic tiles by Maw &
Company, reflecting the restorer William
Burges's interest in medieval floors of this
type. The walls are decorated with hand-
painted tile panels made by W. B. Simpson
& Sons.

ABOVE
Illustration of a thirteenth-century circular
mosaic pavement from the site of Jervaulx
Abbey in Yorkshire. It was discovered in the
nineteenth century, and although it no
longer survives, was published in Henry
Shaw's *Specimens of Tile Pavements* (1858).

Tiles became Gaudí's most expressive architectural medium, and on his buildings ordinary tiles are transformed into something quite unique. He made an astonishing debut with Casa Vicens in Barcelona in the 1880s, where plain and patterned square tiles enhance the decorative character of the villa, with its strong Arabic overtones. The climax to his broken tile work is the early twentieth-century Park Güell, where gatehouses, park benches, and staircases are all richly decorated with mosaic, creating an extraordinarily playful and exuberant atmosphere.

Casa Vicens, 24 Carrer de les Carolines, Barcelona. Plain white and green tiles dominate the upper half of the facade, while floral tiles accentuate the lower half.

numerous fireplaces. They were also used on an outside garden wall leading up to the front door of the house.

Ricardo is a good example of an architect who espoused the use of up-market, hand-painted tiles in houses built for a discerning clientele. He used these tiles mainly inside his houses, which made their enjoyment a private activity. This is in marked contrast to Gaudí, for example, who used ordinary mass-produced tiles in great numbers on the outside of his buildings, where they could be seen and enjoyed by the general public.

Antonio Gaudí began his career in Barcelona in 1878, developing a highly personal style based on a mixture of Catalan Romanesque, Gothic and Moorish sources, combined with touches of Art Nouveau. He soon attracted wealthy and powerful patrons, such as the tile manufacturer Manuel Vicens and the brick manufacturer Eusebi Güell, who allowed him to make his unique architectural visions into reality by commissioning houses and park architecture from him. Barcelona is a centre of tile making, and it was this medium which Gaudí chose to use above all others to emphasize his buildings.

Gaudí's first major commission, from Vicens, was for a house in the Carrer de les Carolines, Barcelona. Casa Vicens was built between 1883 and 1888, and clearly plays on examples of Moorish architecture. Its facade is a successful combination of tiles, stone and wrought iron. Unlike the broken tile mosaic of his later works,

Detail of the lower half of the facade of Casa Vicens, Barcelona. Bands of colourful glazed tiles alternate with recessed areas of stone and brickwork, creating different surface textures.

Detail of the back of a bench in Park Güell. Gaudí used the talents of Joseph Maria Jujol, a specialist in ceramic tile work, for this project.

the facade of Casa Vicens is decorated with un-broken square tiles, whose 'squareness' is further accentuated by a chequer-board pattern of plain green and white tiles, extending over the upper and middle part of the exterior. On the lower part of the house decorative tiles are used. Continuous patterned areas are created by the repeated use of a single tile with a stencilled design of a French marigold in orange and green on a white ground. The effect of the whole is unusual and distinctive, particularly in comparison with its neighbouring buildings.

Between 1886 and 1889 Gaudí built two lodges on the Avinguda de Pedralbes, Barcelona, to serve as an entrance to the estate of the Güell family. The lodges flank a large black

wrought-iron gate with a truly fearsome dragon that repels rather than welcomes the visitor. Each lodge is an asymmetrically arranged building constructed of brick and stone, with a roof made of turrets and towers covered with tiles. The lodges are one of the first examples of Gaudí combining square or rectangular tiles with areas of broken tile mosaic to create varied and lively ceramic surfaces.

One of Gaudí's most celebrated works is the Park Güell, constructed between 1900 and 1904. It is built on the slopes of a hill leading off from Carrer d'Olot, and covers an area of 20 hectares. The park is entered through a gateway flanked by two stone-built lodges with fantastically curved tile mosaic roofs. Two

flights of entrance steps, covered with tiles, then wind their way up to the gardens, on either side of a sculpted tiled dragon. At the top of the steps there is a columned hall, which acts as the platform for the main viewing area above. On the perimeter of the viewing area there is a series of curved benches, also covered with tile mosaic.

Gaudí's use of so much tile mosaic can be explained by the fact that it could cover the curved surfaces of his architecture. Unbroken tiles cannot be used to cover undulating surfaces in any smooth or harmonious way. A closer look at the entrance steps at Park Güell demonstrates quite clearly that Gaudí's tile mosaic is no random affair. The tiles were often broken and then carefully reassembled to fol-

low their original design on the curved surface. In other instances, broken tiles are used to create strictly controlled patterns and forms, for example on the benches of the viewing platform. The general order is reinforced by the symmetrical layout of the park entrance. Variety is achieved by the differing shapes and forms of the two flanking gatehouses, by the myriad effect of the thousands of colourful broken tile pieces, and by surprise elements such as the tiled dragon on the staircase.

Casa Batlló in the Passeig de Gràcia, Barcelona, was built between 1904 and 1906, but was not designed from scratch – the unusual facade and roof were added to an existing building. The undulating facade is covered with a tile mosaic which looks like glazed fish scales, but

Detail of a bench in Park Güell, showing a mosaic of tin-glazed tiles with stencilled decoration.

Buildings by the Dutch architect Hendrikus Petrus Berlage make extensive use of glazed bricks, architectural faience and tiles. Some of these tiles were designed by Berlage himself, such as the sectiel clock-faces on the tower of De Beurs, the Amsterdam stock exchange, but he also employed other artists, particularly for figurative tile pictures. Jan Toorop designed the allegorical panels for the entrance of De Beurs (ABOVE), while Joseph Mendes da Costa made the religious panels for the courtyard of Berlage's Landhuis St Hubertus, near Otterlo. Both Toorop and Mendes da Costa invested their work with complex meanings, underlining various symbolic aspects of Berlage's architecture.

LEFT
Hand-painted panel of tin-glazed tiles on the facade of the American Hotel, Amsterdam, designed by Willem Kromhout in 1902.

most striking of all is the roof, with its strongly curved ridges, ventilation shafts and chimney pots.

The tiles used by Gaudí were ordinary products, tin glazed, and with stencilled or painted designs. They were common throughout Spain at this period. It is the unusual use this architect made of them that lifts his buildings out of the ordinary.

In Holland, Willem Kromhout and Hendrikus Petrus Berlage also made tiles an integral part of their buildings. Kromhout built the remarkable American Hotel in the centre of Amsterdam in 1902. Constructed of yellow brick and finished with natural stone, it also incorporates extensive figurative Art Nouveau tiling made by the Friesian firm of van Hulst in Harlingen. Their buff colour, painted in various shades of green, harmonizes well with the sand-coloured bricks of the building.

Berlage was the most outstanding Dutch architect of the period, with a unique and uncompromising sense of design that made him a formidable figure. His fame rests mainly on De Beurs, the Amsterdam stock exchange, built between 1898 and 1903. Severe brick walls finished with natural stone make up the outside, and are topped by a tower with two large ceramic dial plates, bearing edifying mottoes. It was executed in the sectiel technique, a speciality of De Porceleyne Fles in Delft. The novelty of this technique lay in the fact that the tiles were not square, but cut into shapes that followed the main lines of the design, in much the same

Tile panel at the entrance to De Beurs in Amsterdam, showing an allegory of labour, commerce and industry. It was designed by Jan Toorop in 1902. The sectiel tiles were made by the firm of De Porceleyne Fles in Delft.

way as the glass is cut for a stained-glass window. Each piece was made of porcelain paste to which a particular colour was given by means of porcelain slip. It was strong, frost-proof and well-suited for external use. In the interior of the building, glazed coloured bricks and tiled murals were used. The entrance hall walls are decorated with figurative panels by the Dutch artist Jan Toorop, representing allegorical scenes of Dutch history, labour and industry. These were also executed in sectiel tiling.

Other works by Berlage warrant examination because of the way in which tiles decorated with lettering are integrated with the form of the building. In 1898 he designed a brick villa for the director of the insurance company 'De Nederlanden' in The Hague. The name of his patron, Carel Henny, was laid in the entrance hall in white tiles against a background of black. The square shape of the tiles

has been utilized in such a way that very modern-looking sanserif capital letters with bold, square proportions result. Tiled texts (now destroyed) also found a place in the headquarters Berlage built for the Diamond Workers' Union in Amsterdam in 1898. One of the inscriptions in the entrance hall read, appropriately, *PROLETATIERS ALLER LANDEN VEREENIGT U* ('Workers of the world unite').

Berlage's Landhuis St Hubertus (St Hubert's Lodge), built as a private house between 1914 and 1920 near Otterlo, in what is now the National Park de Hoge Veluwe, for the wealthy Kröller-Müller family, is an unusual building of great merit. The layout of the building represents the head and antlers of a stag, and is a reference to the legend of St Hubert, who was said to have been converted to Christianity when a stag appeared before him with a crucifix between its antlers. The lodge is brick-built and overlooks an artificial lake. In its entrance court there is a clock with a ceramic dial face and two tile panels designed by Mendes da Costa, representing scenes from the legend. The interior of the lodge has glazed brick walls with plain and mosaic tiles on the floor, while glazed bricks and more mosaic tiles were used on the coffered ceilings. The use of these interior tiles is sober and subtle. The positioning of the furniture, which was also designed by Berlage, together with Henri van de Velde, was carefully related to the design of the tiled floors. In the entrance hall, for example, the furniture was custom-built in such a way that the legs fit the pattern on the floor exactly.

In Paris the architects Hector Guimard and Auguste Perret used tiles in contrasting ways for their buildings. Guimard was strongly influenced by Art Nouveau, as can be seen from his extraordinary entrance to Castel Bérenger

Tile panel in the courtyard of the Landhuis St Hubertus (1920). It was designed by Mendes da Costa and shows St Hubert and the stag. The tiles are made of red terracotta, with the background cut away and filled with a green glaze.

Ceramic clock-face above the dog kennel in the courtyard of Berlage's Landhuis St Hubertus.

(1897–8), on the rue la Fontaine. The entrance gate, made of carved stone with whiplash-style Art Nouveau metalwork, gives way to a porch decorated with large, glazed ceramic relief tiles of various shapes. The tiles are both delineated and held in place by metal strips. The sinuous, amorphous, abstract designs on the tiles are a perfect complement to the complex shapes of the metal entrance gate and its surrounding stonework.

Perret, on the other hand, was a rationalist designer who used square concrete frames for many of his buildings. His block of flats on the rue Franklin in Paris, built in 1903, has two entrances above which rise projecting window bays. Between the window bays there is a recessed space with balconies. The whole facade is covered with a tile mosaic that has prominent leaf motifs. These combine to form dense areas

of flat foliage. There is a rigorous control of all the architectural elements, in great contrast to the more undisciplined Art Nouveau forms of Guimard.

The Austrian architect Otto Wagner was another innovator, as his famous Postsparkassenamt (Post Office Savings Bank) in Vienna of 1904 still testifies. Less well-known, but more interesting in its use of tiles, is his 'Majolika Haus' in Vienna, built in 1898. A block of flats built over shops, its facade is completely covered with tiles showing swirling floral Art Nouveau motifs. Again in Vienna, the architect Max Fabiani built a large shop with flats above for the firm of Portois and Fix in 1897. The facade is also completely tiled, but the designs are extremely simple and geometric, much more in tune with the emerging modern outlook and a far cry from the Art Nouveau 'whiplash' designs used by Wagner.

On the Fulham Road in London there is an unusual landmark built in 1910 by the French architect François Espinasse for the Michelin Tyre Company. The overall design of the Michelin Building has been classified as proto-Art Deco. It is extensively decorated with architectural ceramics by Burmantofts of Leeds, and with tile panels depicting the history of motor racing, made by the Paris firm of Gilardoni Fils et Cie. It is gaudy, but possesses an exuberance which makes it impressive.

The architects and designers of the turn of the century often showed that it was of no real consequence whether machine-made or hand-made tiles were used – what mattered was the quality of design and the creative use made of tiles within architectural settings. After the First World War, new outlooks emerged which had great consequences for twentieth-century architecture and design, and for the use of tiles.

LEFT
Art Nouveau tiles in the entrance to Castel Bérenger, 14 rue la Fontaine, Paris. Designed by Hector Guimard, 1897–8.

5

THE NEW WORLD
Susan Tunick

In an article entitled 'The Craft of Tile-Making and Its Relation to Architecture', published in 1915, J. H. Dulles Allen stated that 'Beauty . . . is not a question of mere shapes, but is the evidence of mind acting properly on material.' This precept lies behind much of the beauty and diversity of American decorative tiles. From 1870 onwards, a succession of skilful, creative, determined individuals have helped to shape the American tile industry, although during its first thirty years, artistic and technical knowledge from Europe also had a powerful influence. The industry grew rapidly, especially after the Philadelphia International Centennial Exhibition of 1876, where many fine examples of European and Oriental ceramic wares were on display. These works generated great interest, and the strong desire among American ceramicists to develop products of their own with which to rival them. This desire was to be fulfilled within the next ten years.

After 1900, an increasing number of American-trained technicians and designers entered the field of ceramics, resulting in the production of more innovative tiles. Leadership in the industry passed from large manufacturers to smaller ceramic firms, whose varied styles and techniques changed and diversified the look of American tiles. Advances in glaze technology and experimental production methods led to the creation of unique designs and architectural installations. Handcrafted tiles, inspired by a broad spectrum of historical motifs, ranging from medieval to Mayan, were introduced by these companies. Unfortunately, the Depression of 1929 brought the entire construction industry to an abrupt halt, and many of these small, innovative tile companies were forced out of business. After 1930, few decorative tiles were produced; the vast majority of tiles manufactured in the United States after that date were intended for strictly utilitarian purposes.

THE EARLY YEARS (1870–1900)

In the early years, American tiles owed much to the venerable British tile tradition. More than a hundred British firms were operating between the years 1870 and 1910, and many of the larger manufacturers maintained agents in principal cities overseas. In the 1880s, as the demand for tiles increased enormously, the number of foreign agents grew – Maw & Company was represented in Canada, the United States, South Africa, Australia and New Zealand, as well as in India and the Orient. Outstanding examples of imported British tiles can be found in New York City's earliest extant cooperative apartment house, 34 Gramercy Park, built in 1883. Tiles from the firms of Minton, Hollins & Company, T. & R. Boote and Maw & Company can be seen throughout the building, used for fireplaces, floors and step risers. The beautiful Maw tiles in the outer lobby were designed to look like mosaic tiles, requiring a discerning eye to appreciate that they are only impressed with a mosaic pattern.

The Philadelphia Exhibition of 1876 had been a turning point in the development of an American tile industry. Charles Thomas Davis, in his famous treatise of 1884, *Manufacture of Bricks, Tiles and Terra-Cotta*, made the following observation: 'Nothing in the history of pottery is so remarkable as the progress which has been made in the manufacture of encaustic and decorative tiles, but especially in the latter, in this country since the Centennial Exposition of 1876 . . . [it] injected into us as a nation new conceptions of the ideal, the natural, and the beautiful in art.' Between 1870 and 1900, more than twenty-five companies producing floor and wall tiles were in operation, many of them set up in the years immediately after the Exhibition. Although some survived for a few years only, they succeeded in taking over much of the American market, minimizing the need for imported goods.

Among the most important companies established during this period were the American Encaustic Tile Company, the United States Encaustic Tile Company, Low Art Tile, Trent Tile, the Providential Tile Works, Beaver Falls Art Tile, Cambridge Art Tile, the Robertson Art Tile Company and the Mosaic Tile Company.

Most of the tiles produced by American companies between 1870 and 1900 were largely

OPPOSITE
Tiles by Cambridge Art Tile of Covington, Kentucky (1887–1929).

conservative in design, imitating motifs that were popular in Victorian Britain. Antique, exotic, sentimental and anecdotal subject matter was frequently used. Examples include a tile by the Hamilton Tile Works (1883–96), which depicts a reclining female figure in antique dress, representing 'Poetry', with a winged boy holding a tablet inscribed with the names Homer, Virgil and Dante. Another, made by the Cambridge Tile Manufacturing Company (1890–95), portrays a woman dressed in an elaborate hunting costume and holding a falcon and whip, with a dog at her side. This willingness to follow European fashions stemmed from the tile companies' wish to replace imported tiles with comparable domestic ware.

Many American companies hired excellent modellers, some of whom had been trained in Europe, and who brought with them artistic and technical expertise. William Gallimore, a modeller trained in Britain and Ireland, went to work for the Trent Tile Company in 1886. Herman Carl Mueller, a gifted sculptor who worked at the American Encaustic Tile Company, the Mosaic Tile Company, the National Tile Company and the Robertson Art Tile Company, was educated in Germany. Isaac Broome, who had been born in Canada, skilfully modelled classical subjects for the Trent Tile Company, beginning in 1883, and later joined the Providential Tile Works. However, although tiles produced by American companies were often finely modelled, and displayed technical ability, significant stylistic or mechanical innovations during this period were rare.

Against this, Low Art Tile of Chelsea, Massachusetts (1878–1907), stands out as an exception. John Gardner Low had been born in Chelsea in 1835, and as a young man studied painting and drawing in Paris. Upon his return to America, he became the principal decorator for the Chelsea Keramic Art Works. This early pottery had extremely high standards of decorating, glazing and craftsmanship, which Low carried into his own company. He also invented a unique method of decorating tiles, which he called 'natural process'. Natural objects such as leaves and grasses were pressed into a clay model, producing motifs that were both ornamental and realistic. Low then made a die from this original, which was used to repeat the design on other tiles. In addition, Low Art Tile produced another unusual type of tile decoration, called 'plastic sketches'. These were modelled in low relief, and cast in plaster moulds for varied and repeated use. Arthur Osborne, a young British-trained artist, was responsible for these finely executed images, depicting portraits, animals and scenes such as rural American landscapes.

In 1880, only a year after it had fired its first kilns, Low Art Tile was invited to exhibit at

'Natural process' tile by Low Art Tile.

ABOVE
'Plastic sketch' tile by
Arthur Osborne, with a
portrait of Benjamin
Franklin. Manufactured by
Low Art Tile, 1880–90.

RIGHT
High-relief, hand-
modelled tile, marked
J. & J. G. Low. It appears
to have been made for an
architectural setting. The
matt glazes and sculptural
detail make it a very
unusual example of this
company's work.

Crewe, near Stoke-on-Trent, where it won the gold medal for the best collection of British or American tiles. This is probably the first award ever given to American ceramics in an international competition. According to Lura Watkins, in her article 'Low's Art Tiles', reviews in London newspapers offered the company high praise. Mr Low was credited with inventing ' . . . a new species of Keramic ware', and his work was ' . . . not an imitation of Della Robbia, [whose ceramics influenced many American designers] but a fresh departure.' The following observation by C. A. Wellington is quoted:

They are not striving to imitate or reproduce anything but, in an entirely new field they are resolved to go on and make the best thing that can be made. Ideas come with experience, and with experience only can the mechanical and chemical obstacles be overcome. In this respect they have had no precedent. They have not, like the British manufacturer of today had the benefit of acquired facilities and mechanical experience, although several years study in Europe, under the ablest masters, has brought an artistic knowledge which, for this kind of work, is of even greater value. But there is one element that is still greater than all – that of courage.

Low Art Tile refused to hire men who had worked for other tile companies, and concentrated its efforts on producing a limited number of highly original styles. According to *Pottery and Porcelain of the United States* (1893), it did not produce ' . . . hand-painted, mosaic, printed, encaustic or floor tiles.' Nonetheless, the tiles that it did produce were widely imitated, both in America and overseas.

With a few exceptions, such as Low Art Tile's 'plastic sketches', virtually all American tiles of this period were made using the British technique of dust pressing. Recognizing the significance of this method, which forced a tremendous visual uniformity on the products made using it, is crucial in appreciating the changes that occurred in the American tile industry between 1900 and 1930. The turn of the century brought a new artistic sensibility to the decorative arts, one that advocated a hand-wrought aesthetic above all else. Around this time, an important shift also occurred in the type of company that made decorative tiles, with smaller, craft-oriented potteries beginning to produce a wide variety of tiles from plastic clay. This was in marked contrast to the earlier companies, who had relied on mass production methods to satisfy a market used to buying foreign products.

HAND-CRAFTED TILES (1900–1930)

By 1900, with a new generation of technicians and designers who had been trained in American potteries and art schools, the influence of Europe was considerably diminished. In the years that followed, a remarkable range of American tiles was produced by small companies, where success depended on individuals giving their operations distinctive identities and styles. A number of important ceramicists played key roles in this development, including William Henry Grueby, Maria Longworth Nichols, Henry Chapman Mercer, Mary Chase Perry, Ernest Batchelder and Herman Carl Mueller. These tile makers adapted European and Oriental styles and techniques to their own goals of individual artistic expression. Most returned to using malleable clay, abandoning the extremely popular method of

OPPOSITE
The top two tiles, by the Batchelder Tile Company, are made from wet clay and are an interesting contrast to the bottom tiles, which use the dust-pressed technique. Bottom left: Providential Tile Works; bottom right: Kensington Tile Company.

dust pressing, as the wet clay allowed new opportunities for modelling and carving, and experimenting with surface texture. Consequently, tiles were thicker, rougher and more handmade in appearance, qualities which were highly prized by the growing Arts and Crafts movement.

A 1905 article in the magazine *Good House-keeping* makes the following observation: 'For the purposes of decoration it is not always essential nor even desirable that tiles be mechanically perfect: a little irregularity of shape and glaze which will give a variety of colour tone is valuable . . . Sometimes the tiles classed by dealers as seconds lend themselves particularly to certain forms of decoration because of that unevenness which softens and relieves what might otherwise be a mechanical and uninteresting surface.' These hand-crafted tiles were also ideally suited to the newly developed matt and semi-opaque glazes, radical departures from the glossy, translucent glazes that had been so widely used on nineteenth-

century tiles. One of the most famous of these matt glazes was developed by William Henry Grueby, who had first seen the so-called 'dead' glazes on the work of the French ceramicist Auguste Delaherche at the 1893 World Columbian International Exposition in Chicago. Inspired by these, Grueby began to conduct his own experiments, and by 1898 had perfected a thick, rind-like matt glaze which was appropriate for the heavy earthenware bodies of his tiles and art pottery.

The development of matt glazes led to new methods of working, and a fresh approach to tile decoration. Dust-pressed tiles had relied on a free-flowing glaze to enhance their surface patterns. During firing, a glossy glaze would form darker pools in the hollows of a design, while it thinned out nicely to highlight raised areas on the tile. Matt glazes, on the other hand, are characterized by opacity and limited melting, and work best on flatter tiles, in designs with outlines or solid areas of different colours. Consequently, the pictorial realism of early tiles gradually came to be replaced by a more conventionalized, two-dimensional treatment of subjects. This development paralleled the growing popularity of flat design in the graphic arts of the period.

One of the most influential of the new manufacturers was the Rookwood Pottery of Cincinnati, Ohio, which continued in business until 1960. It was founded by Maria Longworth Nichols (1849–1932), the daughter of a wealthy Cincinnati art patron, in 1880. Her experiments in china painting led her to set up a company designed specifically to produce art pottery. Its earliest products were strongly influenced by Nichols's admiration for Japanese ceramics. In 1884 one of the pottery's decorators, Laura Fry, experimented with the use of

Tile decorated with a rook (Rookwood Pottery's trademark). One of a number of items with similar images produced by the company. Maria Longworth Nichols selected the name 'Rookwood' partly because the last syllable reminded her of 'Wedgwood', and partly because of a fond memory of rooks perched on an old oak tree on the property where she was raised.

Rookwood Pottery ceramic plaque in Fulton Street subway station on the Lexington Avenue line in New York, representing Robert Fulton's steamship, the *Clermont*. An original photograph from Rookwood's records exists, showing the clay relief in a wet state. The glaze transformed the finished piece, obscuring the delicate detailing of the waves, paddle wheel and the ship's railing.

an atomizer for glaze application, and the results, in which a smooth, atmospheric transition occurred in the glaze colours, led to a famous line of slip-painted wares with airbrushed backgrounds. In 1889 the Rookwood Pottery was awarded a gold medal at the Universal Exposition in Paris.

In 1902 the company set up an architectural department, headed by W. P. McDonald, which began producing tiles for fireplaces, walls and other interior settings. By 1903, the architectural department had won a large contract from the New York City subway system. This included orders for cornices, number panels, and a series of pictorial plaques. The growth of the department led to the construction of an extension to the pottery building, completed in 1904. Several years later, in 1907, the company produced its first architectural faience catalogue,

featuring over 125 stock items including mouldings, caps, corner pieces, wainscots, brackets and corbels.

The architectural department remained in operation until 1936, and although many installations of its tiles have been demolished, Cincinnati retains some fine examples. These include an exterior installation at the Dixie Terminal, built by Garber & Woodward in 1913, and the lobby in the Carew Tower (Aeschlager, Delano & Aldrich, 1930).

Grueby Faience of Boston, Massachusetts, was another important firm. After his successful experiments with glazes, William Grueby (1867–1925) set up his own company in 1894. Initially it produced only architectural bricks and tiles, but in 1897 the designer George Prentiss Kendrick joined the firm. Kendrick was made responsible for the company's growing line of art pottery, while Grueby himself remained in charge of glaze development. Their works won international acclaim, earning medals at the 1900 International Exposition in Paris, the 1901 Pan-American Exposition in Buffalo, and the 1904 Louisiana Purchase Exposition in St Louis. This widespread success led to an equally widespread imitation of the renowned matt 'Grueby Green' glaze.

In 1907 the Grueby Pottery Company was formed. Although it shared factory space and kilns with the faience company, the two were separate legal entities, and while Grueby's tile-making operation continued to be financially successful, the pottery met with serious difficulties. In 1909 this situation led to the setting-up of the Grueby Faience and Tile Company. After a fire in 1913, the tile works were rebuilt, and remained in operation until 1919, when the company was bought by the C. Pardee Works in Perth Amboy, New Jersey.

Grueby's tiles were used for public and private buildings in many parts of the United States. Important surviving installations include the New York City subway (Heins and Lafarge, 1904–5), the Gregg Free Library, Wilton, New Hampshire (McLean & Wright, 1905–7), the Cathedral of St John the Divine, New York City (Lafarge & Morris, 1909) and numerous houses by the brothers Charles and Henry Greene in California. The well-preserved interior of the Lackawana railway station (Kenneth Murchison, 1908) in Scranton, Pennsylvania, has many fine Grueby murals, depicting various scenes ranging from Niagara Falls to the Brooklyn Bridge.

The Moravian Pottery and Tile Works of Doylestown, Pennsylvania, was originally in business from 1897 to 1969, and returned to operation in 1974. Its founder was Henry Chapman Mercer (1865–1930). Mercer came from a wealthy family, and was privileged both in his education and opportunities for travel. He developed an interest in antiquities, which led him to explore the areas of archaeology, folk art and museum design. He founded the Moravian Pottery and Tile Works to provide an outlet for his experiments with clay. Mercer drew on a wide range of sources for his designs, including the Bible, mythology and medieval history.

These brightly coloured tiles surrounding the entrance of the 1913 Dixie Terminal in Cincinnati, Ohio, were manufactured by the Rookwood Pottery. Original watercolours for this project exist in the pottery archives, now housed at the Cincinnati Historical Society. Great care was taken in hand-painting each of the coloured glazes onto the clay, resulting in finished tiles that are nearly identical to those in the preparatory studies.

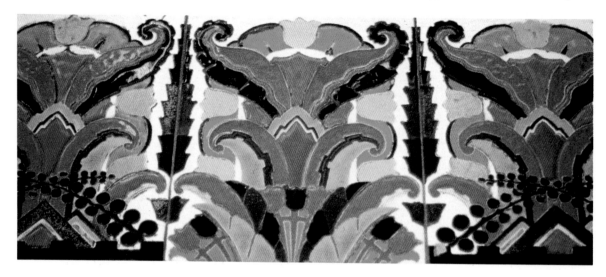

The Moravian Pottery and Tile Works made almost 1500 square metres of tiling for the floors in the great rotunda of the Pennsylvania State Capitol at Harrisburg. Nearly 400 of Mercer's new mosaics were used, including this one, which depicts a Pennsylvania farmer at work in the fields. The commission was one of Mercer's most important, and is one of the finest public works of art in the United States.

The tiles were made from local red and white Jersey clays, and combined exposed areas of clay body with glazed sections, giving them a very rustic quality. Mercer also developed a 'Mosaic' process, for which he obtained a patent in 1902. In this, cut-out clay shapes were fitted together with concrete to create designs. In 1908, Mercer introduced another innovation: 'Brocade' tiles. These were silhouetted shapes, sculpted in high relief, in contrast to his flat mosaics. Each piece was a complete entity – a bunch of grapes, an animal, or a building, for example. They were often set far apart from each other in concrete, which served as a unifying grey background, in a style that developed out of Mercer's interest in the potential of concrete as a decorative material. His tiles were widely used, and can still be seen at the Pennsylvania State Capitol at Harrisburg (Joseph M. Huston, 1904–5), the Chapel at West Point, New York (Cram, Goodhue & Ferguson, 1909) – one of fifteen churches built by these architects, who consistently used Moravian Tiles – and at the Avery Coonley School, Downer's Grove, Illinois (Waldron Faulkner, 1926).

Mary Chase Perry (1867–1961) formed the Pewabic Pottery of Detroit, Michigan, in 1903, in partnership with Horace James Caulkins. Caulkins, owner of the Detroit Dental Depot, had developed the 'Revelation China Kiln' (a compact kerosene-fuelled muffle oven with replaceable parts, a hinged door, and a peephole) for producing dental wares. He believed, correctly, that it could also be used successfully for

'Brocade' tile of Sir Walter Raleigh, designed by Henry Chapman Mercer in 1913. Made of red earthenware with bright polychrome glazes, it is approximately 28 centimetres high.

A panel depicting
'October', designed by
Mercer as a summary
statement of his ideas in a
prototype Mosaic–Brocade
style. It measures
approximately 76×127
centimetres, and was
installed, with similar
panels, on the balcony
overlooking the saloon at
'Fonthill', his house in
Doylestown, in 1929.

RIGHT
Detail of the dramatic tiled exterior of the Guardian Building.

LEFT
Pewabic tiles around a window arch at the Guardian Building.

ABOVE
The Guardian Building in Detroit, Michigan (originally known as the New Union Trust Building), was completed in 1929. The lobby includes striking tiled arches manufactured by the Rookwood Pottery. Although many companies were involved in the ornamentation of this unique skyscraper (including the Pewabic Pottery, Tiffany & Company and the Atlantic Terra Cotta Company), efforts were made to coordinate the colour scheme. Sample tiles, to be used for colour matching, were sent by Mary Chase Perry, owner of the Pewabic Pottery, to Rookwood and to Tiffany's.

ABOVE OPPOSITE
A plaque in the 1918 Canal Street Station (Brooklyn Mass Transit Line) of the New York subway, made by the Mueller Mosaic Tile Company. It was designed by Jay van Everen and is believed to be based on a Lossing-Barrett drawing from 1865. Intended to imitate mosaic, the panel is actually one piece of clay, with grooves between each element of the design.

RIGHT
Detail of the tiles in the majestic Crescent Temple in Trenton, New Jersey, made by the Mueller Mosaic Tile Company. The company made tiles for numerous local buildings.

BELOW OPPOSITE
Tile sample sheet and a copy of the identification chart on its reverse, from the Mueller Mosaic Tile Company. Mueller's company executed numerous large commissions, including work for both the Newark and New York subway systems.

firing clay, and it came to be widely used by many American art potteries.

In 1906, a larger studio was built for the Pewabic Pottery by William Buck Stratton, an architect who later became Mary Chase Perry's husband. Stratton's suggestion that Perry make fireplace tiles for the new home he was building for her subsequently led to the development of Pewabic's architectural tiles. In this, Perry's friendship with the wealthy Detroit art collector, Charles Lang Freer, founder of the Freer Gallery in Washington DC, proved to be invaluable. In addition to introducing her to prominent architects, he made his famous collection of Oriental pottery available to her. This served as the inspiration for Pewabic's unique, iridescent, lustre glaze. Tile commissions were executed for such noted architects as Greene &

Greene, McKim, Mead & White and Eliel Saarinen, who was based at the nearby Cranbrook Academy. Pewabic tiles can be found in buildings in many parts of America, including the Cordelia A. Culbertson House, Pasadena, California (Greene & Greene, 1911), the National Shrine of the Immaculate Conception, Washington, DC (Maginnis & Walch, 1929–44) and St Paul's Protestant Episcopal Cathedral, Detroit, (Ralph A. Cram, 1910–11). In addition, one of the most spectacular skyscrapers in America, Detroit's Guardian Building (Wirt Rowland, of Smith, Hynchman, Grills, 1929) incorporates Pewabic tile murals and polychrome terracotta bands by the Atlantic Terra Cotta Company on its exterior. The building also has striking Rookwood tiles on the lobby walls and ceiling.

In 1961 production at the pottery stopped, and its owner at the time, the Michigan State University, used it instead for purely educational purposes. However, in the early 1980s, an independent, non-profit-making organization called the Pewabic Society, Inc. was set up to resume tile production.

The tile designer Herman Carl Mueller (1858–1941), also set up a manufacturing company, called the Mueller Mosaic Tile Company, in Trenton, New Jersey. Mueller had come to the United States in 1878, after studying art in Germany, in the hope of establishing himself as a sculptor. Finding this difficult, from 1879 to 1885 he utilized his skills by working as a modeller at several art potteries, including the Kensington Art Tile Company in Newport, Kentucky, and the Matt Morgan Art Pottery in Cincinnati, Ohio. In 1886 he began work for the Indiana Terra Cotta Company, where he designed sculptures for the State Capitol in Indianapolis. The following year he went to

work for the American Encaustic Tile Company, where he stayed until 1893, when he left to set up his own business with Karl Langenbeck, a ceramic chemist who had joined the company in 1890. The two men had devised a way to create mosaic-style tile murals using new and faster technology, and were actively involved in all phases of the operation of their company until 1903, when both resigned.

Mueller moved to Trenton, where he set up the Mueller Mosaic Tile Company in 1908. The firm produced a wide variety of hand-crafted tiles and terracotta. It manufactured mosaic-style ceramic plaques for the 1918 extension of the New York City subway system, and Mueller helped introduce tiles into the concrete exteriors of many subway stations of this era. He directed the advertising for his tiles toward the architectural profession, and is known to have worked with architects on the use of tile and concrete for building exteriors. Important installations by the company include the Kelsey Memorial Building at the Trenton School of Industrial Art (Cass Gilbert, 1910), the Crescent Temple, Trenton (1929), the Walker–Gordon Laboratory Plant, Plainsboro', New Jersey (1928–30), and four tile murals for the WPA (Works Progress Administration, a government-funded work-creation scheme), designed by Domenico Mortellito for the Newark subway system (1935).

Ernest Allan Batchelder (1875–1957) was another important designer of tiles who set up his own company. The Batchelder Tile Company was founded in 1909, but Batchelder had been actively involved in the Arts and Crafts movement long before this date. He had directed the Department of Arts and Crafts at Throop Polytechnic Institute in Pasadena, and written widely on the subject of design. When

he left Throop in 1909, he built a kiln behind his home in Pasadena and began to produce decorative tiles. His designs owe much to Grueby and Mercer, but his handling of the clay resulted in tiles with a clearly individual style. Batchelder's floor tiles, for example, are uniformly moulded, and although they have an earthy quality and matt glaze, are more refined than Mercer's. Batchelder's most popular motifs include Mayan designs, birds, foliage and geometric abstracts.

Batchelder architectural tiles met with great success, and the company moved twice, expanding each time. Its tiles appear on the walls and floors of many New York City apartment house lobbies, and can be found in shops, restaurants, swimming pools and hotels throughout the United States. One of Batchelder's last and largest projects was the Hershey Hotel in Hershey, Pennsylvania, built by the famous chocolate manufacturer in 1930, in order to give jobs to many local residents who would otherwise have been unemployed during the Depression. Batchelder tiles were used on the walls, floors and stair risers of a dazzling fountain room, complete with central pool and a mezzanine level. Unfortunately, Batchelder's company, which had employed 150 men at its peak, was itself forced out of business by the Depression in 1932, although Batchelder continued to make pottery in a small shop in Pasadena until the early 1950s.

In addition to the Batchelder Tile Company, there were numerous other California tile manufacturers. The abundant local clays, inexpensive fuel and power and cheap labour were all factors that contributed to an active tile industry, while the rapidly growing population led to a continual demand for new buildings. Moreover, the most popular local architectural

Detail of the Batchelder tiled fountain in the centre of the elaborate tiled room at the Hershey Hotel. The room also retains a number of original small tables with inset Batchelder tiled tops.

OPPOSITE
Detail of a Batchelder tiled floor in the two-storey tiled fountain room at the Hershey Hotel, Hershey, Pennsylvania. The building makes lavish use of tiling throughout, and its construction undoubtedly kept many craftsmen in business during the Depression.

ABOVE
A brilliantly coloured
gable decoration at La
Casa Grande by California
Faience.

LEFT
One of two twin towers at
La Casa Grande in San
Simeon, California, with
tiles by California Faience.

RIGHT
Tiles by the Malibu
Potteries, in the kitchen of
the Adamson Beach
House. The top of the
table has also been tiled,
to coordinate with the
floor, the dado and the
clock.

LEFT AND BELOW
Tiles by Gladding McBean
& Company on the
exterior of the Paramount
Theater in Oakland,
California.

styles, such as Spanish, Mediterranean and Colonial Revival, used large amounts of tile.

One of the most important Californian tile companies was the Malibu Potteries. Although it was in operation for only six years (1926–32), it produced many of the most exquisitely coloured and patterned tiles to be found in California. Rufus B. Keeler, who built and operated the plant for its owner, May K. Rindge, on whose ranch the pottery had first been established, was one of the outstanding ceramicists of the West Coast. Malibu Potteries became a sizable operation, employing up to 127 workers, and carrying a full range of tiles for almost every architectural purpose, both interior and exterior. Examples of Malibu Potteries' tiles can be found in the Los Angeles City Hall (Austin, Parkinson and Martin, 1926–8) and in the Adamson Beach House, Laguna Beach, California (Stiles Clements, 1929), which is now preserved as a museum.

Another particularly interesting company, California Faience, was formed in 1916 by William Bragdon and C. R. Thomas. The firm employed only four or five workers, who produced tiles by pressing clay into incised plaster moulds. This method resulted in distinctive tiles, with fine raised lines dividing the surface. The lines served to keep the company's characteristically bright glazes from running together during firing. Production ceased after 1930, but resumed again in 1932. A number of other ceramic enterprises used the same facilities as California Faience, and Bragdon continued to operate the factory until the early 1950s. Gladding McBean & Company, originally established in 1875 near Sacramento as a sewer pipe and terracotta manufacturer, also acquired three tile works in southern California, in Los Angeles, Glendale and Santa Monica. During the 1920s the company became the largest clay products manufacturer west of the Mississippi Valley. Its tile works were responsible for a wide variety of excellent architectural installations, ranging from the striking Paramount Theater at Oakland, California (Miller & Pfluger, 1930–31), to the Pima County Courthouse, Tucson, Arizona (1930), to the extremely elaborate Los Angeles City Hall, where the company's tiles were used alongside those made by the Malibu Potteries.

TILES IN ARCHITECTURAL SETTINGS

The use of interior tiles in the United States during the 1870s coincided with the introduction of unglazed architectural terracotta for building exteriors. Glazed polychrome ornament suitable for exteriors was not successfully manufactured until 1900, the year McKim, Mead & Whites' Madison Square Presbyterian Church was completed. This church's richly coloured terracotta received wide praise, and the growing popularity of glazed tile and terracotta was reflected in a *New York Times* article of 1907, entitled 'Colour Spreads Glories on City's Architecture'.

New York architects have discovered another medium of artistic expression. The monotony of dull grey and red buildings and miles of brown sandstone and marble are being broken into with colours of brilliant hue. Blues and yellows are appearing on the city's skyscrapers: green, rose, and gold tint her domes and towers. Manhattan, having exhausted all styles of architecture, now paints them, with colours of an Oriental richness. The materials used for this new ornamentation are coloured terra cotta, tiles and faience. When the clays and glazes are

Detail of the restored tile mural on the upper storeys of the Gainsborough Studios at 222 Central Park South, New York City. The mural can be seen from blocks away.

properly combined and fired they produce one of the most imperishable of building materials, with the richness of marble or bronze and admitting of an infinite variety of colour schemes.

Glazed tiles were first used on the exterior of buildings in New York that had been erected for a specific artistic purpose. Perhaps the earliest such example is the Gainsborough Studios (1907–8), a twelve-storey apartment house on Central Park South, with double height artists' studios and duplex living units. This cooperative building, designed by Charles W. Buckham, was planned for a group of successful artists who wished to live in a building with a novel artistic facade. In addition to a terracotta cornice, stone friezes and a bust of Gainsborough, the upper floors have a bold geometric mural composed of red, green, blue, brown and grey Moravian tiles. Nearly 10,000 tiles were needed for this vast design, which extends from the eleventh to the fifteenth floor. According to the record books at the Mercer Archives, they cost $831.68.

In contrast to the overall geometric pattern of the Gainsborough mural, George and Edward Blum used tiles on the outside of buildings in a very different manner. The Blums, New York architects active from 1910 to 1929, first used handmade tiles on an apartment house at 241 West 108th Street. Built in 1910, its facade combined chequer-board Grueby tiles with patterned brickwork to create unusual,

Detail of the tile, brick and terracotta cornice at 730 Riverside Drive, New York City, an apartment house built by George and Edward Blum in 1912. Grueby tiles of various patterns are incorporated into the facade, creating a rich and complex surface.

interwoven, tapestry-like surfaces. During the next seven years, the Blums integrated Grueby and Moravian tiles into the brick and terracotta exteriors of many of their innovative apartment houses. They also incorporated many of these same tiles into the lobbies, hallways and fireplaces of the buildings.

In the early years of the twentieth century, another exterior method of using tiles was being explored in the United States. Referred to in the 1908 *Real Estate Record and Builders Guide* as 'ceramic mosaic incrustation', it combined tiles with concrete facades, and was introduced simultaneously in Paris by the architect Auguste Perret. An important supporter of this method was the Philadelphia firm of Price & McLanahan, which had begun to use Moravian

tiles as colour highlights in concrete building facades in 1903. The Jacob Reed's Sons Store (1903–4), one of the first commercial uses of reinforced concrete in Philadelphia, had Mercer tiles and pictorial roundels incorporated into its brick and concrete exterior. The interior included concrete columns with Mercer tile capitals. Price & McLanahan also used this method in building two large hotels in Atlantic City, the Marlboro–Blenheim (1905) and the Traymore (1907–9). In a 1906 article, Price stated that ' . . . [as a result of] some beautiful colour obtained with Mercer tile, [they] secured sufficient colour and variety to make a building essentially plain in wall-surface give a sense of richness not always obtained by the use of elaborate or expensive ornamental

Detail of the facade of the
American Encaustic Tile
Company building at 16
East 41st Street. In *The
Architect*, July 1929, an
article by Uffington
Valentine refers to this
building, describing
' . . . its faience-covered
facade broadly banded at
the base in turquoise
green surmounted by a
warm ochre shade . . .
[which add] their rich
harmonious tones to an
ensemble that voices the
color-soul of the Orient.'

OPPOSITE
A view of the American
Encaustic Tile Company
building at 16 East 41st
Street, New York City,
showing the company's
tiles as well as
architectural terracotta
made by the Atlantic Terra
Cotta Company. Leon
Solon, Frederick Rhead
and Loiz Rhead, all
important figures in
ceramics, were responsible
for the design of interior
and exterior tiles used in
this building.

work in stone or terra cotta.' Tiles from the
Grueby Faience Company were also used in the
Marlboro–Blenheim. The incrustation technique continued to gain in popularity, and the
1908 *Real Estate Record and Builders Guide* refers
to the fact that the bricklayers' unions were
demanding that they, rather than actual tilers,
be used to install tile in concrete buildings.

Both Mercer and Herman Mueller were
advocates of this technique. (The two were
later to meet, in 1923, and became friends).
Mercer used it extensively in 1908, when he
began to experiment with concrete at 'Fonthill', his idiosyncratic home in Doylestown.
Mueller encouraged its use in the extension of
New York City's subways, by urging the archi-
tect-designer, Squire J. Vickers, to ornament
the new concrete elevated stations with handmade tiles. In a 1919 article Vickers wrote 'If a
little colour be needed, enrich the rough and
rigid surface with bands or plaques of tile . . . It
may be used with restraint to soften a facade
even as a piece of tapestry tempers a wall of
stone, or if it be desired to emphasize any
feature a plaque of joyous brilliant colour may
be placed which will shine resplendent like a
rich jewel roughly set.' This combination of tile
and concrete continued to be used throughout
the mid-1920s, especially in factory buildings.
An outstanding example is the 1926 Frank G.
Shattuck Building. Located on 22nd Street between 5th and 6th Avenues, New York City, it
has boldly coloured geometric tile patterns
above the symmetrical entrances, and on both

of the setback areas of the upper level.

The American Encaustic Tile Company building, at 16 East 41st Street, New York City, also has a fine facade combining tile and concrete. The building, which was originally residential, was modernized to suit the needs of the tile company, and photographs from the early 1920s show that sculptural glazed ornament was used around the windows and doorway, while patterns of tile were set into concrete in the facade above. By 1930, the street-level facade was completely covered in brightly coloured tiles, while the upper storeys remained unchanged. This method of updating facades had been used in New York for a number of years, and can be seen in two rowhouses on East 19th Street, which were redesigned by architect Frederick Sterner to create a small artistic enclave near Gramercy Park. In 1908, Moravian tiles were used by Sterner around the entrance to his own home at 139 East 19th Street, and in the following year he used similar tiles at 135 East 19th Street.

A single Mercer tile, 'The Knight of Nuremberg', one of several set into a massive brick fireplace in the lobby of the apartment house at 780 Riverside Drive, New York City. Built in 1914 by George and Edward Blum, a total of 140 Mercer tiles were used on its lobby and facade.

The use of concrete and tile in residential structures was a phenomenon also seen in rural areas. One particularly remarkable example is the Cordelia A. Culbertson House, built in Pasadena by Charles and Henry Greene in 1911. After years of using wood and shingle, Greene & Greene developed an interest in using gunite – a thin layer of fine-quality concrete blown at high pressure to form an exterior skin on a building. According to *Greene & Greene, Architecture as a Fine Art*, gunite, plaster and various clay products were used in the Culbertson house to produce one of the most sculptural structures ever built by these gifted architects. The ceramic details of the exterior were produced by five of the most important manufacturers of the period, and include floral and solid Grueby tiles inset into the surrounding walkways, figurative column capitals with crouching musicians by the Batchelder Tile Company and red and green rustic roof tiles by Ludowici Celadon (a well-known roof tile company which is still operating in New Lexington, Ohio). The grounds and garden of the house were further ornamented with numerous large-scale planters and small clay animals made by Gladding McBean & Company, and a courtyard fountain with patterned tiles came from the Pewabic Pottery. The architects' interest in tiles can be seen in earlier Greene & Greene houses, including two in Pasadena, the Blacker House (1907) and the Gamble House (1908), where Grueby tiles are used in a most unusual and highly decorative manner for the fireplaces. They were cut into tiny mosaic pieces, which were then set into the bed of solid tiles surrounding the hearth. The mosaic pieces had been glazed with an iridescent lustre, and almost give the appearance of an inlay of mother-of-pearl.

The fireproof qualities of tile made it a suitable facing for the fireplaces and hearths which were central to Arts and Crafts interiors, whether in a Greene & Greene house or in a Blum brothers apartment. *Manufacture of Bricks, Tiles and Terra-Cotta* makes the following comment: 'There are peculiar attractions in decorative tiles: pave a hearth, face a chimney piece or jambs with them, then light a fire in the grate and in the winter's evening enjoy the magical effect, the changing play of light and shadow, and the various portions of the designs relieve monotony, and exert a soothing influence upon all and the chimney corner becomes a home school for refinement in thought, in feeling and in expression.' Handsome tile fireplaces can be found in several New York apartment buildings by George and Edward Blum. Built in 1914, the Vauxhall, at 780 Riverside Drive, has a rustic lobby with a massive brick and tile fireplace. Many of the Mercer tiles used in it portray medieval themes such as castles and knights on horseback. A second apartment house, 780 West End Avenue (1912), no longer has its original Grueby tiles on the lobby floors, but apartments with Grueby tile fireplaces still remain. It is interesting to note that again the theme chosen by the Blum brothers is a medieval one – a knight on horseback.

More extensive interior use of tiles can be found in many of the hotels built in the United States in the early part of the twentieth century. Tiles served a utilitarian function in kitchens, bathrooms and hallways, as well as a decorative one in elegant lobbies, restaurants and bars. In a 1913 article entitled 'The Use of Tile in Interior Finish and Decoration of Hotels', the author states that 'The flexibility of the potter's clay in the hands of the artist modeler, supplemented by the varied palette of the worker in ceramic, can scarcely be limited in the variety of the results obtainable. French decorators of the *Art Nouveau* School have reveled in the *Gres flammes* of [Alexander] Bigot and the architectural faience of Emile Mueller. Our own artists have not yet strayed far from the traditional models. . .' This perceptive comment is best appreciated by comparing the unique handling of clay ornament in Paris with the more conservative American treatment. Many American architects studied in Paris between 1904 and 1914, the period when some of the most significant ceramic facades and lobbies were being designed by Alexander Bigot and Emile Mueller, but it appears these had little impact on the way in which most American architects used glazed tile and terracotta.

The architect F. M. Andrews was responsible for some of the most interesting ceramic interiors in American hotels of the period. Tiles manufactured by the Rookwood Pottery were used by him in the Rathskeller of the Seelbach

Detail showing a central fireplace tile from one of the apartments at 780 West End Avenue, New York City, by the Grueby Faience Company. The Blum brothers chose a medieval theme for these fireplaces as well as for that in the lobby of 780 Riverside Drive, where tiles by Mercer's Moravian Pottery and Tile Works were used.

Hotel in Louisville, Kentucky, built in 1905 (Moravian tiles were used elsewhere in the hotel, which is now protected by its listing on the National Register of Historic Places), the Grand Cafe in the Hotel Sinton, Cincinnati (destroyed, but some murals were donated to the Cincinnati Art Museum) and the Della Robbia Room in the Vanderbilt Hotel, New York City, built in 1912 (this large room was destroyed in 1967, but a small room known as the Della Robbia Bar remains intact and displays the same fine Rookwood ornament).

One of the most ambitious interior uses of tile can be found in the New York City subway system. The original stations, dating from 1904, have rich and varied ceramic ornament. The Rookwood Pottery supplied pictorial plaques and belt coursing for a number of these stations, as did the Grueby Faience Company, the American Encaustic Tile Company and the Atlantic Terra Cotta Company. A particularly handsome Rookwood plaque can be found at Wall Street Station. It depicts the wooden wall from which the street gets its name, a Dutch dwelling and two pine trees. A fence, first ordered in 1644 by Governor Wilhelmus Kieft, was replaced with this much more imposing wooden wall in 1653 by Governor Peter Stuy-vesant. Many of the first stations, constructed nearly ninety years ago, also include ceramic mosaic borders and plaques, supplied by the American Encaustic Tile Company. Stations constructed during the 1918 extension continued to use ceramic tiles from a variety of companies, including the Mueller Mosaic Tile Company. The warmth, richness and durability of their designs, manufactured by some of the finest tile companies in the United States, are now preserved as designated New York City Landmarks.

Although more than sixty years have passed since the Great Depression led to the demise of most of the smaller tile companies in the United States, a remarkable number of their tile installations have survived. In addition, the renewed interest of the architectural profession in colour, texture and surface has led to an increasing use of tiles in contemporary design. Many small tile producers have appeared in recent years, and the variety and quality of their handmade wares is impressive. The growing popularity of newly made tiles, and the increasingly active efforts being made to preserve historic installations, should help to protect the past and guarantee the future of tiles in the New World.

6
THE MODERN AGE

The mass manufacture of Art Nouveau tiles had been the last episode in the first machine age of decorative tile making. After the First World War, there was a more pragmatic approach to tile production, dictated by changed economic circumstances and different kinds of demand. The interwar period saw the development of Modernism in architecture and design, and the emergence of Art Deco. These affected both how tiles were designed and the purposes for which they were used. After the Second World War, screen printing became an important new method of decorating tiles; and the period also saw the involvement of several avant-garde artists in tile design. Highly sophisticated production

The Tekne range of tiles was designed by Daniele Bedini for the Italian firm of Ceramica Bardelli. It is a subtle range of simple relief tiles, which can be augmented with plain tiles where necessary. The example shown here uses two different designs to create a series of plain and patterned diagonal bands.

Set of four tiles designed by Alessandro Mendini in 1983 for Ceramica Pecchiolli in Florence. The design shows a Post-Modernist playfulness, with small pieces of coloured ceramic crossing the divisions of the tiles.

Illustration from a British builder's manual of *circa* 1920, showing a tiler at work.

methods ensured tiles of a uniform quality became available for a mass market. Conversely, from the early 1980s onwards, there has been a renewed interest in old tiles, one manifestation of which has been the recreation of designs from past eras, such as Victorian and Art Nouveau. A new generation of tile artists and newly established tile pottery studios have become active. The modern age, when looked at as a whole, is therefore one of great diversity and contradiction in the production and use of tiles.

THE INTERWAR PERIOD

All Europe was affected by the First World War, if not directly by the conflict, then by its detrimental effect upon trade. Britain, Germany and France had to streamline and rationalize their industries to sustain the war effort, and since little was built in these countries between 1914 and 1918, the demand for tiles fell sharply. When production started up again, a leaner, more cost-effective industry made greater use of automation and prefabrication to increase output with lower labour costs.

During the interwar period, tile presses, which had previously been operated by hand or steam, were automated by the use of electricity. In 1937, Richards Tiles Ltd of Stoke-on-Trent had 140 tile presses in operation, half of which were semi-automatic, while the other half were either fully automatic or still operated by hand. The introduction of tunnel kilns after the war allowed for non-stop tile production. These continuous kilns have a stationary firing zone where temperatures are strictly controlled. The tiles travel through the kiln stacked on trolleys which run on rails. The outcome of the firing was now more guaranteed than ever.

Much of the demand during the interwar period lay with the housing industry. A great deal of mass housing was built during the 1920s and 1930s, as many estates in Germany, Holland, Britain and France still testify. The private housing industry also boomed, particularly during the 1930s when materials and labour were cheap. Plain tiles were needed for kitchens, bathrooms and hallways, and the demand was met by such firms as Boizenburg in Germany, Boch Frères in Belgium, De Sphinx in Holland, and Carter & Company in Britain.

On the Continent, homes were mainly heated by metal stoves or central heating, whereas in Britain, the open fireplace continued to be used. This was catered for by the many manufacturers who put 'slabbed' fireplaces on the market. 'Slabbing' was a form of prefabrication which consisted of bedding tiles on plaster or concrete. It was done either by the tile manufacturer or by builders' merchants. These slabbed panels could be fixed into position by workmen other than skilled tilers.

The interwar fashion was for plain or mottled eggshell tiling, with occasional insets of decorative tiles. These ornamental tiles could be decorated with machine-pressed relief designs, stencilled patterns or hand-painted pictures. However, the demand for decorative tiles had dropped dramatically. The extent to which the picture tile business had shrunk can be seen from the fact that Carter & Company, in Poole, Dorset, had half a dozen picture tile series in production in the 1930s, by designers such as Harold Stabler and Dora Batty, compared with the more than sixty-five picture tile series being made by Minton, Hollins & Company of Stoke-on-Trent during the 1880s.

The fashion for plain surfaces also led to the development of non-ceramic materials which served the same purpose as tiles. Until the

LADIES'
PAPERS

LEFT
The De Stijl artist Theo van Doesburg designed the tiled floor for the entrance hall and first landing of De Vonk in 1918. His watercolour design is made up of buff, black and white squares, which create complex abstract patterns, and each tile was carefully laid according to this plan.

BELOW
Theo van Doesburg designed glazed brick panels to decorate the main entrance of De Vonk between 1917 and 1919. The abstract arrangement of rectangular forms corresponds closely to van Doesburg's own geometrical abstract paintings of the time, and exemplifies the interest of the De Stijl group in non-objective form.

Lettering in tiles above the entrance to the First Church of Christ, Scientist on Ban Straat in The Hague. The bold, square, sans-serif capitals were designed by Piet Zwart in 1926 to blend in with the rectangular architectural form of the church.

beginning of the twentieth century, glazed tiles had been the best type of washable surface, but during the 1920s and 1930s other materials came onto the market and began to compete with tiles. Various fibre or hardboard wall panels, with hard, lustrous, glossy surfaces were produced, which could be installed in kitchens and bathrooms quickly and easily. There was also competition from non-ceramic tiles, made from a special hydraulically pressed aggregate.

Greater automation and prefabrication meant more uniformity, in most European countries, in tile design. The geometric abstract paintings of Malevich and Mondrian, and the fashion for clean outlines and strong colours influenced the work of avant-garde groups across Europe to the same effect. These included the Dutch De Stijl, Russian Constructivists and German Bauhaus artists.

The De Stijl movement was founded in 1917 and continued until 1931. The leader of the group was Theo van Doesburg, while the painter Piet Mondrian and the architect Johannes Oud were among the original members. They propagated an aesthetic of elementary form and basic colour schemes in art, architecture and design, and shunned any kind of figuration. Among their projects was a holiday home for factory girls, on which van Doesburg cooperated with Oud. The house, called 'De Vonk', was commissioned by the social reformer Emilie Knappart. It was built at the coastal resort of Noordwijkerhout and was finished in 1919. Van Doesburg was responsible for the decoration, and designed panels of coloured glazed bricks which were set in the exterior wall, above and beside the central doorway. For the entrance hall and the landing of the first floor he designed a tiled floor made up

of differently coloured, plain machine-made tiles. This was no random arrangement, as a watercolour sketch of the design was made first, and shows every single tile in its final position. The floor blends with the carefully calculated colour schemes of the interior.

The Modernists' emphasis on creating plain surfaces with materials such as tiles, glass, marble, brick and concrete, as part of a simplified geometric architecture, became known as the 'International Style'. The Gemeentemuseum in The Hague, built in 1935, is a good example. It was designed by Berlage, who in his old age was still capable of creating something startlingly modern. It has a concrete frame covered with brick on the outside, a flat roof with low horizontal lines and an exterior with the emphasis throughout on rectangular form. Inside, extensive areas of plain coloured tiles are used for

Individual, hand-decorated tiles, made by the firm of Dunsmore in 1929, decorate the ground floor of St Anne's Flats, Doric Way, London.

Bernard Leach tiles in the fireplace of a private house in Scalby, Scarborough, built in 1929. The tiles are stoneware, with animal, landscape and patterned motifs, alternating with others that are plain buff-grey. The design of the tree suggests a Japanese influence, while the animals are simple, bold and strong, reminiscent of primitive art.

ABOVE
Detail of the neo-Egyptian architectural ceramics and tiles on the Art Deco facade of a cinema in the Essex Road, Islington, London. The bold, flat forms and strong colours of Egyptian art were a popular source for many Art Deco designers.

LEFT
Tiles on the exterior of the Tuschinski Theatre, Reguliersbreestraat, Amsterdam, designed by H. L. de Jong between 1918 and 1921. The tiles and architectural ceramics were made by Plateelbakkerij Delft in Hilversum, and feature a blend of semi-figurative and abstract forms. The strong angularity of the fragmented shapes is reminiscent of Cubism.

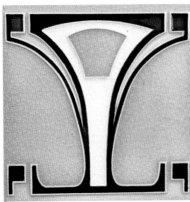

TOP
Art Deco tiles at the entrance of the
New Inn, The Market, Selby.
Manufactured by Candy Tiles,
Newton Abbot, *circa* 1930.

ABOVE
German Art Deco tile made by
Boizenburg Wandplattenfabrik *circa*
1925, with a machine-pressed
abstract motif.

RIGHT
Set of Art Deco tiles with tube-lined
decorations, made by Maw &
Company, *circa* 1935. Geometric
motifs predominate, but designs with
sailing ships were also popular.

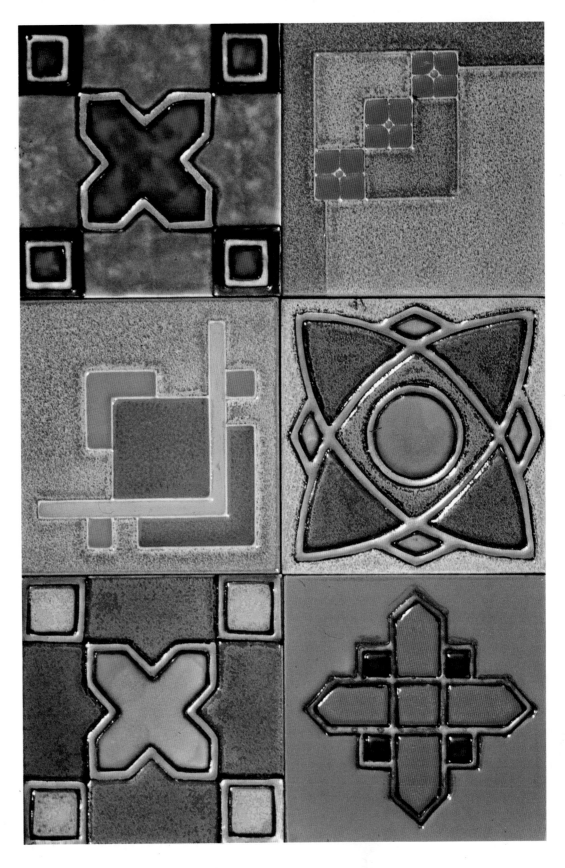

RIGHT
Detail of the facade of the
Santa Ana factory in
Triana, Seville. The factory
was founded in 1870, but
new tiles, painted by
A. Kiernam, were installed
in the early 1950s on the
lower half of the exterior.
This scene shows cherubs
filling a kiln.

FAR RIGHT
The Fábrica de Conservas
(jam factory) at Catarroja,
Valencia, built *circa* 1925.
This building, with its
remarkable tiled front,
now stands derelict and
seems to be facing an
uncertain future. Don
Quixote and Sancho Panza
were part of the firm's
registered trademark.

OPPOSITE LEFT
Tile panel at the Mercado
de Colón, Calle de Jorge
Juan, Valencia.

OPPOSITE RIGHT
Hand-painted panel,
originally used at branches
of Maypole Dairies. Made
by Pilkingtons, *circa* 1920.

the floors and walls of the entrance hall, and for
the staircases and corridors, thus creating a
functional but clinical interior.

The strict functionalism of the International
Style was offset by another interwar design
phenomenon: Art Deco. This term (an abbre-
viation of the French 'Arts Décoratifs') was bor-
rowed from the influential Paris *Exposition
Internationale des Arts Décoratifs et Industriels
Modernes* of 1925. Although the exhibition pavilions were often of great architectural interest,
the focus was clearly on the industrial and decorative arts. These were not overtly mechan-
istic, but were rather individual designs,
demonstrating that handmade work still com-
manded prestige. Art Deco influenced architecture, interior and product design. Tiles began to
show patterns with squares, triangles and
circles, in strong, bright colours. Because so few

decorative tiles were made, it was possible to decorate them by hand, using techniques such as slip-trailing, stencilling, and painting. Strong colour combinations, for example black with orange and gold, were not uncommon.

Art Deco was not, however, purely geometrical. It also allowed for a kind of streamlined figurative design, incorporating both curvilinear and rectilinear shapes, in which there were echoes of Cubism and even Oriental art. An extraordinary building of this kind is the Tuschinski Theatre in Amsterdam, built by the architect H. L. de Jong between 1918 and 1921. The facade of glazed faience has exotic features such as elephants' heads, but also includes relief tiles with Cubist configurations. In Valencia the Mercado de Colón (vegetable market), built in 1925, is another fine example of Art Deco architecture. It successfully combines glass and metalwork with brick, stone, architectural

Two screen-printed tiles designed by Reginald Till in 1953.

ceramics, decorative tiles and mosaic.

The International Style and Art Deco represent only two facets of interwar design. In Britain there had been only limited acceptance of these new trends, and their influence is generally seen only in the design of public buildings such as cinemas, schools, factories and seaside pavilions. An interest in the past continued, as can be seen in the neo-Tudor architecture which became popular in the 1930s, particularly for houses in the new suburbs. A similar preoccupation with the past can be seen in Spain. A neo-Moorish railway station was built in Toledo in the early 1930s, complete with Moorish-style *cuenca* tiles in the interior. In 1929 Seville hosted the Ibero-American Exhibition, and redesigned the Parque de Maria Louisa to house the exhibition stands. Many of these impressive neo-Baroque buildings remain, containing an abundance of tiling decorated with naturalistically painted scenes. All this happily ignored any kind of modern trend.

POST-SECOND WORLD WAR DEVELOPMENTS

After the Second World War, Modernism in architecture crystallized in the 1950s and 1960s to become what is now known as 'Brutalism'. This type of architecture took as its model the rational but radical and uncompromising designs of Mies van der Rohe and Le Corbusier. Reinforced concrete, steel and plate glass were the characteristic materials of this style. Many older buildings, especially in town centres, were demolished to make way for high-rise flats, stores, office blocks and multi-storey car parks. On the domestic front, brick-built houses of rather bland and uniform design appeared. Little external decoration was used,

and the tiles that were needed were mostly plain, and included for functional reasons.

In Britain, during the period of austerity immediately after the Second World War, decorative tile making was at a low ebb. It was not until the early 1950s that this situation changed. The tiled fireplace in particular once more became the focus of attention in the domestic interior, and was used to add pattern and colour to interior design. The architect Mark Hartland Thomas wrote in *Design* magazine no. 56 in 1953:

Tiled fireplaces are normally 'slabbed-up' by the builders' merchant, who buys an assortment of tiles and assembles them on concrete backing. They are offered as ready-made 'surrounds' to house builders and house owners. They are mostly of dreary design, with little opportunity for the public to choose anything better, except from the few merchants who now offer a simple frame for the mantelpiece with a wide range of patterned or coloured tiles from which the customer can choose. This way of selling tiles should now increase, because it offers variety to the customer and is backed by some of the leading tile makers who are employing first-class designers and producing some very charming decorated tiles. The method will lead customers of both kinds, householders and architects, to rediscover the possibilities of tiling for decoration in many different situations and in large areas as well as small.

These leading manufacturers included Pilkington Tiles and Carter & Company, as well as some smaller firms such as the Purbeck Decorative Tile Company, who did not make their

Tiled bench on the Plaza de España, Seville, 1929. Dedicated to the Spanish province of Barcelona, it is decorated with a scene depicting the return of Christopher Columbus to Spain in 1493. He is shown making his report of the discovery of America to Ferdinand and Isabella, whose court was in Barcelona at that time.

RIGHT
Chickens roasting outside a shop in the Carrer dels Escudellers, Barcelona. The tiles, which were probably made *circa* 1920, provide a fireproof surface, reflect heat on to the food being cooked and embellish the appearance of the oven.

FAR RIGHT
Hand-painted, slip-trailed tiled advertisement in Seville for Rioja wine, dated 1925.

H.IJ.S.M. 10 JUNI. 1874.

N.S. 3. JUNI. 1946.

AANGEBODEN·DOOR·DE·V.V.V.·BAARNS·BLOEI
NAMENS·DE·INWONERS·VAN·BAARN·TER·HERDENKING
INBEDRIJFSTELLING·ELECTR.·TRACTIE·OP·X·1946.

BAARN

AMSTERDAM

Tile panel on Platform One of Baarn railway station, Holland, celebrating the 1946 electrification of the Baarn–Amsterdam line.

own tiles, but specialized in decorating blanks. The new medium of the 1950s and 1960s was screen printing, which allowed for bold patterns and flat colour, and coincided with the ideas of Modernism, particularly prevalent during this period. Change and progress in all aspects of design were highly valued, and most new tile designs were abstract, based around one or two basic units from which a number of different extended patterns could be created. Designers of note at that time were Peggy Angus, who worked for Carter & Company, and Reginald Till, who designed both for Carters and for Purbeck.

After 1945, a new generation of avant-garde artists became involved with tile design. Pablo Picasso began painting tiles and pottery during the 1950s and 1960s after meeting Georges Ramié, who ran a pottery in Vallauris in the south of France. Picasso's tiles were decorated with scenes of Spanish bullfights and erotic fantasies. Salvador Dali turned his attention to tiles in the early 1950s, when he created six colourful designs on the themes of love and music, war and peace, and life and death. They demonstrate Dali's ability to encapsulate important elemental themes in memorable pictorial form.

Other artists such as Henri Matisse, Joan Miró, Victor Pasmore, Bart van der Leck and

Detail of a large tile panel, situated on the exterior wall of the DDR Haus der Ministerien in what was East Berlin. Designed by Max Lingner, and made by the Meissen State Porcelain factory in 1952, it depicts idealized scenes of socialist life, celebrating the glories of the former German Democratic Republic. The whole panel is 24.2 metres long and 3 metres high.

Maurits Escher also created tiles and panels for specific architectural projects. Matisse became interested in ceramic mural decoration when he was working on the Chapelle du Rosaire of the Dominican sisters at Vence, near Nice, in 1947. He had been asked to make designs for the interior, which included not only stained-glass windows, but also tile panels. A panel at the east end of the chapel depicts the fourteen stations of the Cross in a single composition. On an adjacent wall is a representation of the Virgin and Child in simple outlines, while a third panel, over 5.4 metres high, was placed behind the altar and shows the figure of St Dominic. Matisse not only provided the designs, but also

painted all the compositions directly onto the unglazed tiles, after which they were glazed and fired by a professional potter.

Pasmore designed a tiled mural for the Regatta Restaurant on the South Bank, built in 1951. He said 'The design was conceived, in collaboration with Gibson, the architect, essentially as a function of the architecture. Its purpose was: to echo at the back of the building the organic forms of the tree at the side, thus emphasizing the unity of the restaurant and garden; to break up the closed well caused by the inclusion of the bridge stairway within the perimeter of the building and to allow [a] continuously mobile viewpoint at close quarters.'

phous black lines and coloured shapes, painted in red, blue, yellow and green. Miró also made ceramic tile panels for Harvard University in 1961, and a ceramic mural for the Guggenheim Museum in 1967.

The work of the Dutch printmaker Escher has many connections with tiles. In 1936, during a study trip to Spain, he spent time at the Alhambra studying the principles of tile tessellation. He made copies of the Moorish tile mosaics and used these examples of alternating and contrasting shapes and colours to solve the problem of 'periodic space-filling' in his own prints, where figurative black-and-white shapes alternate, leaving no spaces in between. On this subject he wrote 'The Moors were masters in the filling of a surface with congruent figures and left no gaps over.' In the

In 1952 the East German artist Max Lingner created a huge tile panel for the then DDR Haus der Ministerien in East Berlin. It is a good example of Communist propaganda, celebrating the achievements of the Marxist state and executed in a Socialist Realist style. Within a similar Socialist vein are the enormous tile panels created by Rolando Sá Nogueira and Maria Keil in 1959 for the Avenida Infante Santo, Lisbon. They form the background to staircases which lead to large housing estates, and celebrate aspects of the all-important Portuguese fishing industry.

In 1955 the Surrealist artist Joan Miró was commissioned to make two tiled walls for the UNESCO headquarters in Paris. This three-year project was executed in cooperation with the ceramic artist José Artigas. The works are known as the Wall of the Sun and the Wall of the Moon, and are decorated with Miró's amor-

Miró's Wall of the Moon
for the UNESCO building
in Paris, created in a
collaboration with the
ceramic artist José Artigas,
and installed in 1958.

Panel designed by Bart van der Leck for the VARA broadcasting studio, Hilversum, Holland. The tiles were made by De Porceleyne Fles in Delft, and represent the new dawn of the working class.

1950s and 1960s Escher made designs for tiled columns of alternating shapes of fish and birds. These were used in the entrance halls of two schools, one in The Hague in 1959, the other in Baarn in 1968. These columns, with their bold black-and-white shapes, add a touch of visual interest to the sterile modern entrances of the schools.

Another Dutch artist who worked with tiles was Bart van der Leck. He had been involved with van Doesburg and Mondrian in the De Stijl movement in 1918, where he developed a style of severe abstraction, in which naturalistic forms were reduced to barely recognizable shapes made up of triangles and rectangles. Van der Leck worked in this style throughout his life, and just before his death in 1958 designed a large tile panel in bright primary colours, which was placed on the outside of the VARA broadcasting studio in Hilversum in 1961.

Reactions against Modernism set in from the 1970s onwards, and during the past fifteen years there has been a return to ornamentation and figuration, part of the general Post-Modernist trend in art and design. It has also influenced tile design. One manifestation of this has been the revival of Victorian and Art Nouveau designs. Major firms have brought out printed tile ranges that copy Victorian and Art Nouveau examples directly, or have launched sets of hand-painted tiles imitating the work of Morris and De Morgan. These tiles are an interesting phenomenon, but not necessarily an example of good creativity in design. Luckily

Panel by Maggie Angus Berkowitz entitled 'Riving Slate, Elterwater Quarry', made in 1982 for the entrance of the head office of Burlington Slate in Coniston. The figures are outlined in black and the colours built up with multi-fired layers of glazes, creating a rich surface texture.

LEFT
Panel of screen-printed tiles created by the Italian firm of Marazzi in 1988.

BELOW
Relief panel and a set of six relief tiles from Marlborough Ceramics' glazed terracotta range (1992).

RIGHT
Tiled walls in an interior designed by Alessandro Mendini in 1991. Mendini worked with Ettore Sottsass in the experimental Studio Alchymia in Milan in the late 1970s, and moved on the fringes of Memphis, the innovatory Italian design group, during the 1980s. His work is flashy, playful, colourful and decorative.

ABOVE
Set of four screen-printed wall tiles designed by Gio' Ponti in 1958 for Ceramica Gabbianelli in Milan. The design can be manipulated to create a range of different patterns.

LEFT
A range of computer-designed, screen-printed tiles created in 1988 by the Purbeck Decorative Tile Company. Computer-aided design means tiles can be custom-made from the outset. The tile decorated with lions is based on a medieval example.

BELOW
Screen-printed tile designed by Ettore Sottsass in 1968 for Ceramica Cedit in Milan. The black and white pattern epitomizes the abstract designs popular during the 1960s.

Maw & Company panel at McDonald's Burger Bar in the St John's Centre, Leeds, installed in 1985.

the revival of interest in ornamentation has also encouraged many young artists and designers to turn their attention to the making and decorating of tiles, and it is the latter that is proving to be a more promising development.

At the present moment the tile market seems to have polarized. On the one hand a market has been created for a more discerning, wealthier customer, and in Britain this demand, mainly for the domestic market, is being filled by an increasing number of small potteries and studios, specializing in the production of hand-crafted, well-designed tiles. Some very diverse and creative work is being done in this field, ranging from handmade medieval-style, and hand-painted neo-delft tiles, to slip-trailed and screen-printed tiles. New firms such as

Marlborough Ceramics, Palm Pottery, Art on Tiles, New Castle Delft, Cheshire Medieval Ceramics and The Life Enhancing Tile Company all cater for this market.

On the other hand, there is the mass-produced tile for popular consumption, which is very much a part of the growing D.I.Y. business. Machine-made tiles are thinner and lighter than ever before, with exactly the same size and thickness. Easy-to-use tiling tools, adhesives and grouts are now available, and enable D.I.Y. enthusiasts to install tiles in their homes. Major British firms such as H. & R. Johnson and Pilkington Tiles are competing with overseas manufacturers such as the Italian firms Marazzi and Aurelia Ceramiche, who put mass-produced tiles with a touch of designer

OPPOSITE
La Torre Arcobaleno, on via Forlanini, Milan. Designed by the Architectural Division of the Original Designers SR5 Studio, Milan, it was created by the firms of Marazzi (tiles), Mapei (tile adhesive) and Tempini (marketing), in 1990. The scheme gave an old water tower a new skin, and is part of attempts being made to regenerate the area around the Porta Garibaldi station.

During the past decade, many artists throughout Europe have been given the opportunity of putting their ideas concerning tile design into practice in the underground stations of major cities. Tiles are still the best surface to withstand the wear and tear inflicted by millions of travellers, as well as creating stimulating visual environments and putting art on display in public places. Many underground stations now have bright and cheerful platforms, where the functional and decorative aspects of tiling are combined.

Screen-printed tiled maze by the design partnership Crosby, Fletcher and Forbes, on the Victoria Line platform at Warren Street underground station, London.

RIGHT
Tiling in the Alto Dos Moinhos underground station, Lisbon, designed by Júlio Pomar in 1989.

BELOW
The new tiles in the Richard-Wagner-Platz underground station, Berlin.

BOTTOM
The 'Metropolitana' underground station in Rome, opened in 1990. It is tiled with so-called 'klinker tiles', produced by the Italian firm of Laria, whose hardness enables them to withstand heavy wear.

The fire station at Choisy-le-Roi, designed by Jean-Luc le Petit and Jean Zunz of Groupe Daviel, and completed in 1990, is decorated with brightly coloured red and blue tiles.

flair on the market. The Spanish tile industry now dominates much of the European tile market, and has been one of the business success stories of recent years, with Gres De Nules, Artemarmol and Ceramicas Gaya among the leading firms.

Contemporary artists have managed to create designs that are both innovative and suitable for mass production. Since 1981 London Underground has embarked on an extensive programme of refurbishment at many stations, in which tiling plays a prominent part. What is happening now is not new. London Underground has carried out major tiling programmes at various times throughout the twentieth century, but the present scheme is distinguished by the origination of particular identities for many stations, with the artists' designs reflecting aspects of life, commerce or the

history of the area in the immediate vicinity of the station; and this is something that has not been seen before.

The use of tiles as a functional wall covering is now a part of the structure of underground rail networks in many European cities. Apart from London, one of the most exciting projects currently being undertaken is in Lisbon, where a number of artists such as Vieira da Silva, Rolando Sá Nogueira and Júlio Pomar have, during the past few years, created decorative schemes for new suburban underground stations. This has been done with the involvement of the well-established Lisbon tile factory of Viúva Lamego.

The past ten years have seen the abandonment of Modernism and its penchant for bare concrete, glass and steel. Post-Modernist buildings still use concrete or steel frames, but their

Lycée de l'Image et du Son, Angoulême, France, built in 1990 by the architect Jean-Jacques Morisseau. Combi-Colour tiles by Gail-Inax AG have been used on the exterior.

RIGHT
The administration
building of the Stinnes
Baumärkte at Esslingen in
Germany, designed by
Hans Auras in 1991. The
facade is covered with tiles
from Gail-Inax AG's
Combi-Colour range, here
creating a gigantic red
colourfield.

OPPOSITE
The interior of the Stinnes
Baumärkte at Esslingen.
The same red tiles used on
the exterior here blend in
well with the overall
interior colour scheme.

Detail of a hand-decorated
tile panel by Jan
O'Highway, entitled
'Fantasy Rainforest'
(1987).

exteriors tend to be covered with a material such as brick or tiles. Post-Modern architects, for example Michael Graves, Jean-Jacques Morisseau and Hans Auras, have rediscovered the functional and decorative qualities of tiles, and use them on many of their buildings. The tiles are often plain white or of a single colour, but once extended over a large area they become an important part of the building's visual impact.

In this endeavour the architects are aided by leading European tile manufacturers such as Shaws of Darwen, Villeroy & Boch, Ceramica Bardelli, De Porceleyne Fles and Gail-Inax AG. These firms produce a range of tiles using state-of-the-art technology, thus ensuring that their products are of the highest possible quality. Exterior tiles can now be made that are not only frost proof and abrasion resistant, but also resistant to the effects of acid rain.

Not all innovation is market-led or takes place in the public eye. Other developments have occurred away from prestigious schemes, the interests of big business, fashionable designers or affluent consumers. Tile art inspired by community needs has resulted in some excellent work, created by non-specialists under the guidance of dedicated professionals. One such project was run by the ceramic artist Teena Gould who, during the 1970s and 1980s, was involved with children, adults and ethnic minority groups from Islington, Lambeth, Kennington and Clapham in London, in making tiles for wall decorations in schools and public spaces. One of Gould's aims was to initiate creative responses in order to visually enhance the built environment.

More and more manufacturers, designers and consumers are showing an interest in the innovative use of tiles as part of both traditional and new architecture. The scope for functional application, colour, figuration and pattern are virtually limitless. There is a vast history of diverse examples to draw on, as well as the work of new creative talents who show the way ahead. Tiles as a functional and aesthetic medium have enriched architecture in a multitude of different ways. Present attitudes show a clear concern for preserving what is best from the past, as well as recognizing the need for new creative tile design as an integral part of contemporary architecture.

Community tiling uses the creative energies of local groups under the professional guidance of a trained ceramicist, such as Teena Gould, who was active in a number of projects in London between 1971 and 1988. One of these projects was 'Tiles for Peace' at Swiss Cottage Square, London (1987).

RIGHT
The Immeuble de Logement at 106 rue du Château des Rentiers, Paris. Built in 1986, it was designed by Architecture Studio. The facade features a giant tiled map of the Paris Metro by the firm of Buchtal, Verneuil-sur-Seine.

LEFT
The Circle, opposite Tower Bridge, London, designed by the architects Campbell, Zogolovitch, Wilkinson and Gough, and completed in 1989. These luxury apartments are faced with blue glazed bricks made by Shaws of Darwen, creating a permanent colour accent in the built environment.

View of the platform of the recently completed Rathenau Platz underground station, Nuremberg. The walls have been tiled with giant portraits of the psychologists Jung and Freud.

Bibliography

1 FOR GOD AND EARTHLY PRINCES

Beaulah, Kenneth, 'Medieval Paving Tiles', *Fired Earth – 1000 Years of Tiles in Europe*, Richard Dennis Publications/Tiles & Architectural Ceramics Society, Shepton Beauchamp, 1991

Berendsen, Anne, *Tiles – A General History*, Faber and Faber Ltd, London, 1967

Caiger-Smith, Alan, *Tin-Glaze Pottery*, Faber and Faber Ltd, London, 1973

Deroeux, Didier (ed.), *Terres Cuites Architecturales au Moyen Âge*, Mémoires de la Commission départementale d'Histoire et d'Archéologie du Pas-de-Calais, Arras, 1986 (vol. XXII)

Eames, Elizabeth, *Medieval Tiles – A Handbook*, British Museum Publications Ltd, London, 1968

—— *English Tilers*, British Museum Press, London, 1992

Norton, Christopher, 'Les carreaux de pavage du Moyen Âge de l'abbaye de Saint-Denis', *Bulletin Monumental*, Société Française d'Archéologie, Paris, 1981, II, 139: 69–100

—— 'Medieval Tin-Glazed Painted Tiles in North-West Europe', *Medieval Archaeology*, 1984, XXVIII: 133–72

—— *Carreaux de Pavement du Moyen Âge et de la Renaissance*, Musée Carnavalet, Paris, 1992

Öney, Gönül, *Ceramic Tiles in Islamic Architecture*, Ada Press, Istanbul, 1987

Wight, Jane, *Mediaeval Floor Tiles*, John Baker, London, 1975

2 PAINTED MAGNIFICENCE

Ahlefeldt-Laurvig, Jorgen, 'Tegels van de Fabrieken te Kopenhagen in de 18e Eeuw', *Tegel*, 1974, 3–4: 5–13

Barros Veloso, A. J. and Almasque, I., *Azulejos De Fachada Em Lisboa*, Câmara Municipal de Lisboa, Lisbon, 1988

Becquart, Geneviève, *Carreaux de Faience dans le Nord de la France 1650–1850*, exhibition catalogue, Musée de Saint-Amand-les-Eaux, Saint-Amand-les-Eaux, 1983

Frothingham, Alice Wilson, *Tile Panels of Spain*, Hispanic Society of America, New York, 1969

Gschnitzer, H. and Menardi, H., *Stuben Öfen Hausmodelle*, Haymon-Verlag, Innsbruck, 1986

Honey, W. B., *European Ceramic Art*, Faber and Faber Ltd, London, 1952 (vol. II)

Horne, Jonathan, *English Tin-glazed Tiles*, J. Horne, London, 1989

Jonge, C. H. de, *Dutch Tiles*, Pall Mall Press, London, 1971

Lane, Arthur, *A Guide to the Collection of Tiles*, HMSO, London, 1939

Lemmen, Hans van, *Delftware Tiles*, Shire Publications, Princes Risborough, 1986

Meco, José, *The Art of Azulejo in Portugal*, Bertrand Editora, Amadora, 1988

Meco, J. and Marggraf, R., *Fliesenkultur in Portugal*, Rasch Verlag, Bramsche, 1989

Pluis, J., Akker, M. van den and Muller, H. E., *Dieren op Tegels*, De Tijdstroom, Lochem, 1974

Quinterio, Francesco, *Maiolica Nell' Architettura Del Rinascimento Italiano*, Cantini, Florence, 1990

Rackham, Bernard, *Early Netherlands Maiolica*, Bles, London, 1926

Ray, Anthony, *English Delftware Tiles*, Faber and Faber Ltd, London, 1973

Schaap, Ella, *et al.*, *Dutch Tiles*, exhibition catalogue, Philadelphia Museum of Art, 1984

Stahl, Siegfried, *Deutsche Fliesen*, Klinkhardt & Biermann, Braunschweig, 1977

Wilson, Timothy, *Ceramic Art of the Renaissance*, exhibition catalogue, British Museum, London, 1987

3 THE MARCH OF THE MACHINE

Austwick, J. and Austwick, B., *The Decorated Tile*, Pitman House, London, 1980

Barnard, Julian, *Victorian Ceramic Tiles*, Studio Vista, London, 1972

Beaulah, Kenneth, *Church Tiles of the Nineteenth Century*, Shire Publications, Princes Risborough, 1987

Cartier, Jean and Morrison, Henri, *La Céramique Architecturale des Années 1900 dans le Beauvaisis*, exhibition catalogue, Musée départemental de l'Oise, Beauvais, 1980

Forrer, R. E., *Geschichte der europäischen Fliesenkeramik*, Verlag von Schlesier und Schweikhardt, Strasburg, 1901

Furnival, William J., *Leadless Decorative Tiles, Faience and Mosaic*, Stone, 1904

Kay, Geoffrey, 'Charles Lynam – An Architect of Tile Factories', *Journal of the Tiles and Architectural Ceramics Society*, 1992, 4: 21–8

Lambton, Lucinda, *An Album of Curious Houses*, Chatto & Windus, London, 1988

Lefêvre, Leon, *Architectural Pottery*, Scott Greenwood & Co., London, 1900

Lemmen, Hans van and Skinner, Deborah, *Minton Tiles 1835–1935*, exhibition catalogue, City Museum and Art Gallery, Stoke-on-Trent, 1984

Lemmen, Hans van, *Victorian Tiles*, Shire Publications, Princes Risborough, 1981

Lockett, Terence A., *Collecting Victorian Tiles*, Antique Collectors Club, Woodbridge, 1979

Pearson, Lynn F., *The People's Palaces*, Barracuda Books, Buckingham, 1991

Pitarch, A. José, and Dalmases Balaña, N. de, *Arte e Industria en España 1774–1907*, Editorial Blume, Barcelona, 1982

Scharf, Aaron, *Art and Industry* (Units 33 and 34, A100 Foundation Course), The Open University Press, 1971

Thomas, Thérèse, *Villeroy & Boch 1748–1930*, exhibition catalogue, Rijksmuseum, Amsterdam, 1977

Weisser, Michael, *Jugendstilfliesen*, Fricke Verlag, Frankfurt, 1983

4 THE TRIUMPH OF THE DESIGNER

Barnard, Julian, 'Some Work by W. J. Neatby', *The Connoisseur*, November 1970: 165–9

Broos, Kees, *Architekst*, Lecturis, Eindhoven, 1989

Catleugh, Jon, *William De Morgan Tiles*, Trefoil Books, London, 1983

Greenwood, Martin, *The Designs of William De Morgan*, Richard Dennis and William E. Wiltshire III, Shepton Beauchamp, 1989

Gunnink, Marijke, *St. Hubert's Lodge*, Kröller Müller Foundation, 1985

Kessler-Slotta, Elisabeth, *Max Laeuger*, Saarbrücker Druckerei und Verlag, Saarbrücken, 1985

Sembach, Klaus Jürgen, *Art Nouveau*, Benedikt Taschen Verlag, Cologne, 1991

Lemmen, Hans van, *Minton Hollins Picture Tiles*, Gladstone Pottery Museum, Stoke-on-Trent, 1985 (2nd edn)

——'Art Nouveau Tiling', *Ceramics*, 1986, IV (July/August)

Myers, Richard and Myers, Hilary, 'Morris & Company Ceramic Tiles', *Journal of the Tiles and Architectural Ceramics Society*, 1982, 1: 17–22

Saint, Andrew, *Richard Norman Shaw*, Yale University Press, New Haven, 1976

Stoppani, Leonard, *et al.*, *William Morris & Kelmscott*, The Design Council, London, 1981

Zerbst, Rainer, *Gaudí*, Benedikt Taschen Verlag, Cologne, 1991

5 THE NEW WORLD

Allen, J. H. Dulles, 'The Craft of Tile-Making and Its Relation to Architecture', *Journal of AIA*, January 1915, III, 1: 5

Austwick, J. and Austwick, B., *The Decorated Tile*, Pitman House, London, 1980: 44

Barber, Edwin Atlee, *Pottery and Porcelain of the United States*, G. P. Putnam's Sons, New York, 1893. Reprinted Watkins Glen, New York (Century House Americana), 1971: 353

Barnard, Julian, *Victorian Ceramic Tiles*, Studio Vista, London, 1972: 16

'Color Spreads Glories on City's Architecture', *New York Times*, January 27 1907, Section III: 1

Davis, Charles Thomas, *Manufacture of Bricks, Tiles and Terra-Cotta*, Sampson Low, Marston, Searle and Rivington, London, 1884: 425–6

Dolkart, Andrew Scott and Tunick, Susan, *The Architecture of George & Edward Blum*, 1992 (unpublished MS)

Goulet, Patrice and Goulet, Anne-Laure, 'Paris-Ceramique', *Architecture Interieure Crée*, January 1980, 125: 69–75

Graves, William Hagerman, 'The Use of Tile in the Interior Finish and Decoration of Hotels', *The Architectural Review*, April 1913: 46

LeBoutillier, Addison, 'Tiles in Home Decoration', *Good Housekeeping*, August 1905: 125

Makinson, Randell L., *Greene and Greene, Architecture as a Fine Art*, Peregrine Smith Inc., 1977: 197

Mercer Archives, Spruance Library, Henry Mercer Museum, Bucks County Historical Society, Doylestown

Montgomery, Susan, *The Spirit of the New Idea in Artistic Handicraft: the Ceramics of William H. Grueby*, Boston University, 1990: 437 (unpublished thesis)

Price, William L., 'The Possibilities of Concrete Construction from the Standpoint of Utility and Art', *American Architect*, 7 April 1906, 89: 120

Real Estate Record and Builders Guide, 30 May 1908: 1006

Real Estate Record and Builders Guide, 18 July 1908: 149

Reed, Cleota, *Henry Chapman Mercer and the Moravian Pottery and Tile Works*, University of Pennsylvania Press, Philadelphia, 1987: 83

Saunier, Charles, 'Nouvelles Applications du Grès au Revetement des Façades', *L'Architecte*, 1908, 3: 85

Solon, Leon V., 'The Display Rooms of a Tile Manufactory', *Architectural Record*, November 1922: 368

Stookey, Lee, *Subway Ceramics: A History & Iconography*, New York City, 1992: 86

Taft, Lisa Factor, *Herman Carl Mueller, Architectural Ceramics and the Arts and Crafts Movement*, New Jersey State Museum, Trenton, 1979: 20

Vickers, Squire J., 'Architectural Treatment of Stations on the Dual System of Rapid Transit in New York City', *Architectural Record*, January 1919, XLV: 20

Watkins, Lura, 'Low's Art Tiles', *Antiques*, May 1944, XLV: 250

6 THE MODERN AGE

Blanchett, Chris, 'Picture Tiles in the 20th Century', *Fired Earth – 1000 Years of Tiles in Europe*, Richard Dennis Publications/Tiles and Architectural Ceramics Society, Shepton Beauchamp, 1991

Bruno, Ernst, *The Magic Mirror of M C Escher*, Ballantine Books, New York, 1976

Carter, Cyril and Hidden, H. R., *Wall and Floor Tiling*, Caxton Publishing Co. Ltd, London, 1934

Dupin, Jacques, *Joan Miró – Life and Work*, Thames and Hudson, London, 1962

Hartland Thomas, Mark, 'Tiles', *Design*, August 1953, 56: 19–29

Jacobus, John, *Matisse*, Thames and Hudson Limited, London, 1974

Jencks, Charles, *Modern Movements in Architecture*, Penguin Books, Harmondsworth, 1980

Ramié, Georges, *Céramique de Picasso*, Editions Albin Michel, Paris, 1984

Rasey, Susan, *A Brief History of 'Marlborough' Tiles and Tile Products 1936–1986*, Marlborough Ceramic Tiles, 1987

Scarlett, Frank and Townley, Majorie, *Arts Décoratifs 1925*, Academy Editions, London, 1975

Straaten, Evert van, *Theo van Doesburg*, SDU Publishers, The Hague, 1988

Picture Credits

2 Kea, London/Francesco Venturi
6 Ceramgres, Treviso
8 Leighton House Museum, London
10 Gail-Inax AG, Architektur-Keramik, Giessen, Germany
12 Martin Charles, Middlesex
13 Richard Dennis Publications, Somerset
14 The British Museum, London
15 Musée Sandelin, St-Omer/Claude Theriez
17 Courtesy of the Dean and Chapter of Westminster
18 Hans van Lemmen
19 Hans van Lemmen
20 both Hans van Lemmen
21 Hans van Lemmen
22 Giraudon, Paris
23 Giraudon, Paris
24 both Hans van Lemmen
25 Martin Charles, Middlesex
26 The British Museum, London
27 both Hans van Lemmen
28 both Hans van Lemmen
29 The British Museum, London
30 left Hans van Lemmen
30 right The British Museum, London
31 Hans van Lemmen
32 both Hans van Lemmen
33 Hans van Lemmen
34 both Hans van Lemmen
35 Scala, Florence
36 above Talavera Antiques, London/photo Bridgeman Art Library, London
36 below left Kea, London/Francesco Venturi
36 below right John Bethell Photography, St Albans/Bernard Cox
39 Stedelijke Musea, Bruges
40 Kea, London/Nicolas Sapieha
41 Fitzwilliam Museum, University of Cambridge/photo Bridgeman Art Library, London
42 both International Ceramics Museum, Faenza inv.# 7883
43 above left International Ceramics Museum, Faenza inv.# 21244
43 right International Ceramics Museum, Faenza inv.#7875
43 below left International Ceramics Museum, Faenza inv.# 7890
44 Scala, Florence
45 International Ceramics Museum, Faenza inv.# 6866
46 Scala, Florence
47 Hans van Lemmen
48 left Hans van Lemmen
48 right Kea, London/Francesco Venturi

49 Kea, London/Francesco Venturi
50 both Hans van Lemmen
51 John Bethell Photography, St Albans/Bernard Cox
52 Kea, London/Francesco Venturi
53 above Hans van Lemmen
53 below Kea, London/Francesco Venturi
54 Hans van Lemmen
55 both Kea, London/Francesco Venturi
56 Hans van Lemmen
57 Réunion des Musées Nationaux, Paris
58 left International Ceramics Museum, Faenza inv.# 21365
58 right Réunion des Musées Nationaux, Paris
59 International Ceramics Museum, Faenza inv.# 21610-21613
60 John Bethell Photography, St Albans
61 Hans van Lemmen
62 left Hans van Lemmen
62 right The National Gallery, London
63 National Museum Paleis Het Loo, Apeldoorn/photo A. A. W. Meine Jansen
64 Hans van Lemmen
65 © National Trust 1993, London
66 Jan Pluis, Noordsleen, Holland
67 Hans van Lemmen
68 John Bethell Photography, St Albans
69 John Bethell Photography, St Albans
70 Giraudon, Paris
71 Wilhelm Joliet, Königswinter, Germany
72 Calmann & King Archives
73 Kea, London/Francesco Venturi
75 Kea, London/Nicolas Sapieha
76 Arquivo Nacional de Fotografia, Instituto Português de Museus, Lisbon
77 Arquivo Nacional de Fotografia, Instituto Português de Museus, Lisbon
79 Kea, London/Francesco Venturi
80 left Kea, London/Francesco Venturi
80–81 Arquivo Nacional de Fotografia, Instituto Português de Museus, Lisbon
82 Kea, London/Francesco Venturi
83 Kea, London/Nicolas Sapieha

84 Hans van Lemmen
85 Fitzwilliam Museum, University of Cambridge/photo Bridgeman Art Library, London
86 above Kea, London/Francesco Venturi
86 below Wim Swaan, London
87 both Jan Pluis, Noordsleen, Holland
88 above Hans van Lemmen
88 below Hans van Lemmen
89 Editions D'Art Lys, Versailles
90 left Hans van Lemmen
90 right Kea, London/Francesco Venturi
91 Hans van Lemmen
92 Hans van Lemmen
93 E. T. Archive, London
94 Liverpool City Council
95 Richard Dennis Publications, Somerset
96 Hans van Lemmen
97 Jonathan Horne, London
98 Hans van Lemmen
99 both Hans van Lemmen
100 both Hans van Lemmen
101 John Freeman, London
102 Richard Dennis Publications, Somerset
103 Hans van Lemmen
104 Traditional Homes, London/Ian Parry
105 Traditional Homes, London/Ian Parry
106 left Richard Dennis Publications, Somerset
106–7 The Royal York Hotel
108 Hans van Lemmen
109 © National Trust 1993, London
110 Royal Collection, St James's Palace, © HM The Queen
111 Traditional Homes, London/Ian Parry
112 both J. Sainsbury's PLC, London
113 Arcaid, London/Lucinda Lambton
114 left Louise Irvine, London
115 above Arcaid, London/Lucinda Lambton
115 below Hans van Lemmen
116 above Hans van Lemmen
116 below Calmann & King Archives
117 © National Trust 1993, London
118 above The Ironbridge Gorge Museum, Telford
118 below John Riddy, London
119 John Bethell Photography, St Albans
120 both Arcaid, London/Lucinda Lambton

121 left Hans van Lemmen
121 right Hans van Lemmen
122 Angelo Hornak, London
124 Hans van Lemmen
125 *The World of Interiors*, London
126 Villeroy & Boch Keramik Museum, Mettlach
127 both Hans van Lemmen
128 both Hans van Lemmen
129 left Arcaid, London/Lucinda Lambton
129 right Hans van Lemmen
130 Hans van Lemmen
131 all Hans van Lemmen
132 Hans van Lemmen
133 Jean-Loup Charmet, Paris
134 Kea, London/Francesco Venturi
135 Kea, London/Francesco Venturi
137 Private Collection/Photo Bridgeman Art Library, London
138 left Minton Museum, Royal Doulton, Stoke-on-Trent
138 right Hans van Lemmen
139 Richard Dennis Publications, Somerset
140 The Ironbridge Gorge Museum, Telford
141 Victoria & Albert Museum, London/photo Bridgeman Art Library, London
142 both Hans van Lemmen
143 Queens' College Cambridge
144 Richard Dennis Publications, Somerset
145 Arcaid, London/Lucinda Lambton
146–7 John Freeman, London
148 both Hans van Lemmen
149 Victoria & Albert Museum/photo John Freeman, London
150 Hans van Lemmen
151 John Freeman, London
152 both Hans van Lemmen
153 Hans van Lemmen
154 John Bethell Photography, St Albans
155 Calmann & King Archives
156 Kea, London/Francesco Venturi
157 Kea, London/Francesco Venturi
158 Kea, London/Francesco Venturi
159 Kea, London/Francesco Venturi
160 left Hans van Lemmen
160 right Stichting De Beurs van Berlage, Amsterdam
161 Stichting De Beurs van Berlage, Amsterdam
162 both Hans van Lemmen
163 Hans van Lemmen

164 Angelo Hornak, London
165 John Freeman, London
166 Peter Mauss, ESTO
167 The Newark Museum, New Jersey. Purchase 1919
169 Smithsonian Institution, Washington DC photo no. 9Z-14455
170 Smithsonian Institution, Washington DC photo no. 9Z-14454
171 left The Newark Museum, New Jersey. Purchase 1983 Louis Bamberger Bequest Fund
171 right Carole Zabar Collection, New York City/Peter Mauss, ESTO
173 Malvina Solomon & Company, New York City (top 2 titles)/Peter Mauss, ESTO
174 Carole Zabar Collection, New York City/Peter Mauss, ESTO
175 David Lubarsky, New York City
176 Peter Mauss, ESTO
177 Paul Tunick, New York City
177 The Newark Museum, New Jersey. Purchase 1919
178–9 Cleota Reed, New York/ Courtney Frisse
180 Winslow B. Pope
181 above Susan Tunick, New York City

181 below Winslow B. Pope
182 Susan Tunick, New York City
183 above David Lubarsky, New York City
183 below Friends of Terra Cotta Inc. New York City/Peter Mauss, ESTO
184 Paul Tunick, New York City
185 Paul Tunick, New York City
186 Tile Heritage Foundation, Healdsburg, California
187 left Tile Heritage Foundation, Healdsburg, California
187 right The Malibu Lagoon Museum, California/photo Marc Muench
188 both Mary Swisher, Sacramento, California
190 David Lubarsky, New York City
191 Peter Mauss, ESTO
192 Peter Mauss, ESTO
193 Peter Mauss, ESTO
194 Peter Mauss, ESTO
195 Peter Mauss, ESTO
197 The Seelbach Hotel, Louisville, Kentucky
198 Ceramica Bardelli, Milan
199 International Ceramics Museum, Faenza inv.# 22723
200 E. T. Archive, London
201 Richard Dennis Publications, Somerset

202 above Rijksdienst Beeldende Kunst, The Hague
202 below both Hans van Lemmen
203 both Hans van Lemmen
204 above Angelo Hornak, London
204 below Hans van Lemmen
205 above left Hans van Lemmen
205 centre Hans van Lemmen
205 right The Ironbridge Gorge Museum, Telford
206 both Hans van Lemmen
207 left Hans van Lemmen
207 right Richard Dennis Publications, Somerset
208 Hans van Lemmen
209 above Kea, London/ Francesco Venturi
209 below left Hans van Lemmen
209 below right Kea, London/ Francesco Venturi
210 Hans van Lemmen
211 Hans van Lemmen
212 Hans van Lemmen
213 both Hans van Lemmen
214–15 Unesco, Paris & © DACS, London, 1993
216 Hans van Lemmen
217 Maggie Berkowitz/A. Morris, Craft North 1986
218 above left Ceramica Filippo Marazzi S.P.A., Milan

218 above right Marlborough Ceramics, Wiltshire
218 below Alessandro Mendini, Milan
219 left Purbeck Decorative Tiles Company, London
219 above right International Ceramics Museum, Faenza inv.# 24578
219 below right International Ceramics Museum, Faenza inv.#24502
220 Mapei, Milan
221 Hans van Lemmen
222 London Transport Museum
223 above left Hans van Lemmen
223 right Hans van Lemmen
223 below left Laria Klinker Ceramico, Santena, Turin
224 Archipress, Paris/Boegly
225 Gail-Inax AG, Architektur-Keramik, Giessen, Germany
226 Gail-Inax AG, Architektur-Keramik, Giessen, Germany
227 Gail-Inax AG, Architektur-Keramik, Giessen, Germany
228 Hans van Lemmen
229 Hans van Lemmen
230 Peter Cook, London
231 Archipress, Paris/S. Couturier
232–3 Villeroy & Boch, Mettlach

Index

AALMIS, JAN 67, 67
Abaquesne, Masséot 56, 56, 58
Aerdenhout, Holland: 'Kareol' 152, 153
airbrushed decoration 102
Alcázar, the: altars 47; Palace of Peter the Cruel 31, 31, 32; pavilion of Charles V 47, 50; Salón de Carlos V 50, 50
Alhambra, the 12, 31, 33, 34, 37, 213, 213
Allard, Carel 67
Allen, J. H. Dulles 167
American Encaustic Tile Co. 168, 170, 185, 192, 194, 196
Amsterdam 63, 66, 67, 78; American Hotel 160, 161; De Beurs 160, 161, 161–2; Diamond Workers' Union headquarters 162; house porches 129, 152, 152; Rijksmuseum 47, 123, 123; Tuschinski Theatre 204, 207
Anagni, Italy: Duomo 16
Andrews, F. M. 195
Andries, Frans 50, 61
Andries, Guido (di Savino) 50, 59, 61, 61

Andries, Jasper 63, 84
Andries, Joris 61
Angoulême, France: Lycée 225
Angus, Peggy 210
Ansbach, Germany 86, 87; Residenz 87
Antwerp 50, 59, 61
Apeldoorn, Holland: Paleis Het Loo 63
Architectural Pottery Co. (Poole) 121
Architecture Studio 231
Ardier, Paul 67
Arnhem museum: farmhouse 92
Arraiolos, Portugal: Lóios church 80
Art Deco 163, 199, 204, 205, 206–8
Artemarmol (Spanish firm) 225
Artigas, José 213, 215
Art Nouveau 90, 124, 127, 132, 150, 161, 162–3, 163, 195, 199, 216
Art on Tiles (British firm) 221
Arts and Crafts movement 88, 91, 139, 141, 150, 152, 195
Atlantic City, NJ: Marlboro–Blenheim Hotel 191, 192

Atlantic Terra Cotta Co. (USA) 181, 182, 192, 196
Auneuil, France: Boulenger factory 128, 128, 129
Auras, Hans 226, 229
Aurelia Ceramiche (Italian firm) 221
Avignon, France: Papal Palace 38
Azeitão, Portugal: Quinta da Bacalhoa 74

BAARN, HOLLAND: railway station 210; secondary school 213, 216
Bankel, Georg 124
Barcelona, Spain 56, 88; Avinguda de Pedralbes lodges 158; Carrer dels Escudellers 209; Casa Batlló 135, 159, 161; Casa Vicens 156, 157, 157–8; Park Güell 135, 156, 158, 158–9, 159; Santa Cruz hospital 55, 56; S. Pau del Camp 16
Barco, Gabriel del 80
Barnard, Bishop & Barnard 145
Batchelder, Ernest Allan 172, 185
Batchelder Tile Co. (USA) 172,

185, 185, 194
Batty, Dora 200
Bawsey, Norfolk 29, 29
Beauregard, Château de 67
Beauvais, France 127, 127, 128, 132; la Maison aux Faience 28
Beaver Falls Art Tile (USA) 168
Bedini, Daniele 199
Belfast: Crown Liquor Saloon 108
Benfica, Portugal: Palácio de Fronteira 83
Berkowitz, Maggie Angus 217
Berlage, Hendrikus Petrus 13, 152, 160, 161–2, 162, 203
Berlin: DDR Haus der Ministerien 211, 213
Bernardes, António de Oliveira 78
Best, Mary Ellen 66
Bigot, Alexander 195
Blackpool, England: Winter Gardens 150
Blåtårns Ovnfabrik (Copenhagen) 87
Bloempot, De see De Bloempot
blue-and-white decoration 56, 56, 66, 68, 78, 78, 80, 83, 86, 87, 98, 131

Blum, George and Edward 190–1, *191*, *194*, 195, *195*
Boch, J. F. 123
Boch Frères 128, 200
Bogaerd, Adriaen 61
Boizenburg Wandplattenfabrik 200, *205*
Bologna, Italy: S. Petronio 45
Bolsward, Holland 66
Bolzano, Italy 85
Boote, T. & R. 121, 168
Bordeaux, France: Abbaye de la Sauve Majeure 21
Bosch, Jacobus van den 138, 150, 152, *152*
Boulenger factory (Auneuil) 128, *128*, *129*
Boulton, William 121
Boumeester, Cornelis 78
Bragdon, William 189
Bristol 84, *85*; Everard Building 150
British Museum *15*, *26*, 28, *29*, *30*
Broome, Isaac 170
Brown, Ford Madox *143*
Brühl, Germany: Schloss Falkenlust 71, *71*
'Brutalism' 208
Buchtal (Verneuil-sur-Seine) *231*
Buckham, Charles W. 190
Buckler, J. C. *117*
Burges, William 152–3, *155*
Burgkmair, Hans 85
Burmantofts (Leeds) *106*, *107*, *120*, 150, 163
Burne-Jones, Sir Edward *141*, *141*, *143*
Byland Abbey, N. Yorkshire *20*, 21

CALIFORNIA FAIENCE (USA) *187*, 189
Cambridge Art Tile (Covington, Ky) 168, *168*
Cambridge Tile Manufacturing Co. (USA) 170
Cambridge University: Queens' College *143*
Campbell, Zogolovitch, Wilkinson and Gough (architects) *231*
Campbell Brick and Tile Co. (Stoke) *13*
Candy Tiles (Newton Abbot) *205*
Capua, Italy: Duomo *43*
Cardiff Castle, Wales 153, *155*
Carron Ironworks Co. 113
Carter & Co. (Poole) 145, 200, *200*, 210
Castrup Werk (Amager Is., Denmark) 87
Caulkins, Horace James 177
Ceramica Bardelli (Italy) *199*, 229
Ceramica Cedit (Milan) *219*
Ceramica Gabbianelli (Milan) *219*
Ceramica Pecchiolli (Florence) *199*
Ceramicas Gaya (Spain) 225
Chamberlain, Walter 98–9, 136, 138

Chelsea Keramic Art Works (USA) 170
Chertsey Abbey, Surrey *15*, 24
Cheshire Medieval Ceramics 221
Chislehurst, Kent: St Mary's Church 128
Choisy-le-Roi, France: fire station *224*
Christóbal de Augusta 50, *50*
Christóbal de Augusta 50, *50*
Cincinnati, Ohio: Carew Tower 175; Dixie Terminal 175, *176*; Hotel Sinton 196
Clarendon Palace, nr Salisbury *26*, 27
Coalbrookdale Co. 113
Coimbra, Portugal: Sé Velha 74
Collins and Reynolds (printers) 100, *100*
computer-aided designs *219*
Coniston, England: Burlington Slate *217*
Constância factory (Lisbon) 88
Copyright of Design Act 136
Cordoba, Spain 30, 31
Corn, W. & E. (Staffordshire) 123
'Cosmati' work 16, *16*
Costa, Francisco Jorge da 83
Cottingham, L. N. 98, 99, 138
Crane, Walter 13, 138, 139, *141*
Craven Dunnill (Jackfield) *108*, 121, 123
creamware 98
cuenca tiles 47, *48*, *49*, 50, *50*, 132
cuerda seca tiles 46, 47, *49*
Cuvilliés, François 68, *71*

DAIRIES 67, 84, *110*, 124, *124*, 206
Dali, Salvador 210
Davis, Charles Thomas 168
Day, Lewis F. 136
De Bloempot (Rotterdam) 67, *67*, *71*, 91
Deck, Theodore *129*
Decorative Art Tile Co. Ltd (Stoke) 103
De Distel (Amsterdam) 129
Delaherche, Auguste 174
Delft, Holland 45, 63, 67
Delftfield Pottery (Glasgow) 84
delftware 42, 45; English *38*, *41*, *64*, 84, *84*, *85*, *96*, 98
De Morgan, William 8, 13, *137*, 138, 145, *145*, 148, 150, 153
De Porceleyne Fles (Delft) 129, *131*, 139, 161, *161*, *216*, 229
De Sphinx (Holland) 200
De Stijl movement *202*, 203, 216
Detroit, Mich.: Guardian Building *181*, 182; St Paul's Cathedral 182
Dill, Bartholomaus 85
Doesburg, Theo van *202*, 203, 216
Dorotheenthal factory (Germany) 86
dos Santos, Manuel 78
Doulton & Co. (London) *114*, *118*, 121, 168
Douzies (French firm) 128
Downer's Grove, Ill.: school 177

Doylestown, Penn.: 'Fonthill' *178*, 192
Dresden, Germany 123; Pfund Dairy 124, *124*
Dunn, Henry Treffry 142
Dunsmore (British firm) *203*

EASTLAKE, CHARLES LOCK 113
Eberbach, Germany: Zisterzienser-Abtei 29
Écouen, Château d' 56, *58*
Edinburgh: John Knox's House 67
Eginton, H. 98, *138*
Escher, Maurits 211, 213, *213*, 216
Escofet, Tejara y Cia (Barcelona) 132
Escorial, El 56, *56*
Espinasse, François 163
Esslingen, Germany: Stinnes Baumärkte *226*
Este, Isabella d' *43*, 45, 46
Estoi, Palácio do Visconde de (Portugal) *41*
Eyck, Jan van: *Madonna with Canon George van der Paele* 38, *38*

FABIANI, MAX 163
Faenza, Italy 45; Palazzo Ferniani *43*
faience 42, 45
Fauquez, Jean-Baptiste 59
Febvrier (Lille factory) 59
Fernández, Juan 56, *56*
fireplaces *27*, *30*, *66*, 84, 113, 121, *132*, 142, *143*, *148*, 150, 194, 195, *195*, 200, *203*, 208
Floris, Jan 50, 61
Fountains Abbey, N. Yorkshire 21, *21*
Fourmaintraux (Desvres firm) 88
Frederiksbergslot, Denmark 87
Freer, Charles Lang 182
Fry, Laura 174
Furnival, William J. 105

GAIL-INAX AG *10*, 225, *226*, 229
Gallimore, William 170
Gantner family 85
Gaudí, Antonio 13, *135*, 152, *156*, 157–9
Gilardoni Fils et Cie (Paris) 163, *164*
Giverny, France: Monet's house 88, *88*
Gladding McBean & Co. (Cal.) *188*, 189, 194
glazes and glaze techniques: lead 16, 19, 20, 21, 24, *27*, 30, 38, 105; matt 174, 176; ready-made 103; tin 28, 30, *36*, 37–8, *38*, 42, *56*, *58*, 59, 64, 67, 71, 84, 85, 86, *87*, 88, *88*, 91, 129, 132, 142, *see also* delft; faience; maiolica
Godwin, William Henry 121
Godwin Tile Factory (Lugwardine) 121, *121*

Good Housekeeping 174
Gothic architecture: and floor tiles 19
Gothic Revival, the *13*, 99, 152
Gould, Teena 229, *229*
Granada, Spain 30, 31, *see also* Alhambra
Graves, Michael *10*, 229
Gréber, Charles 127, *127*
Green, Guy 96, *96*
Greene, Charles and Henry 176, 182, 194
Gres De Nules (Spanish firm) 225
Grieksche A factory (Delft) 67
Groupe Daviel *224*
Grueby, William Henry 172, 174, 175, 176
Grueby Faience and Tile Co. (Boston) 175, 176, 190, 191, *191*, 192, 194, *195*, *195*, 196
Grundy, George Henry 102
Guimard, Hector 152, 162–3, *163*

HAARLEM, HOLLAND 63; station *129*
Hague, The: First Church of Christ, Scientist *202*; Gemeentemuseum *203*; villa (Berlage) 162
Hamilton Tile Works (USA) 170
Hampton Court, nr London 67
Harlingen, Holland 63, 66, 88, 91, *92*, 161
Harrisburg, Penn.: State Capitol 177, *177*
Headingley, England: Spring Bank *148*
Herckenrode Abbey, Flanders 61
Hereford, England: Green Dragon Hotel *119*
Hernández, Roque 50
Hershey, Penn.: Hershey Hotel 185, *185*
Hilversum, Holland: house porch *130*; VARA broadcasting studio 216, *216*
Hirschberg palace, Germany 87
Hohensalzburg, Austria *86*
'Holland' tile firm (Utrecht) 150, *152*
Hornsea, North Humberside: 'Farrago' 115
hotels *107*, *119*, *160*, 161, 185, *185*, 191, 192, 195–6, *196*
house porches, entrances and facades 129, *130*, *131*, *132*, 152
Hulst, van *see* van Hulst

IJSSELSTEIN, HOLLAND: church 124, *124*
Iles, Frank 145
Indiana Terra Cotta Co. (USA) 182
Industrial Revolution 13, 91, 95, 96
'in-glaze' decoration 42, *59*
Innsbruck, Austria 85
International Style 203, 206, 208

Irving, Washington: *Tales of the Alhambra* 37
Islamic art *see* Moorish tiles
Iznik tiles (Islamic) *8*, 146, 150

JANSEN, JACOB 63, 84
Jervaulx Abbey, Yorkshire *155*
Johnson, H. & R. 221
Jones, Owen 138
Jong, H. L. de *204*, 207
Jujol, Joseph Maria *158*

KEELER, RUFUS B. 189
Keil, Maria 213, *213*
Kelmscott Manor, Oxfordshire 142
Kendrick, George Prentiss 175
Kensington Art Tile Co. (Ky) *172*, 182
Keyser, Hendrik de *123*
Kiernam, A. *206*
kilns 20, 28, 96, 103, 123, 177, 200
King's Lynn, Norfolk: Clifton House 28
Kleyn, J. F. 91
Kloet, Willem van der 78
Knappart, Emilie 203
Kromhout, Willem 152, *160*, 161

LAEUGER, MAX 138, 152, *153*
Laguna Beach, Calif.: Adamson Beach House *187*, 189
Lamego factory (Lisbon) 88, *90*, 225
Langenbeck, Karl 185
Laria (Italian firm) 222
Leach, Bernard *203*
Leck, Bart van der 210, 216, *216*
Le Comte, Adolf *131*, 138, 139
Leeds: McDonald's *221*; town hall 100
Leeuwarden, Holland 63; station 129
Leighton, Lord Frederick 150
Le Petit, Jean-Luc *224*
Life Enhancing Tile Co. (Britain) 221
Lingner, Max *211*, 213
Lisbon, Portugal 11, 74, 83; Avenida Infante Santo 213, *213*; Madre-de-Deus 74, *76, 77*, 83; Mercês church 78; Nossa Senhora church 78; Paço Saldanha 83; Palácio Nacional de Sintra, Sintra, nr Lisbon 74; Real Fábrica do Rato (royal tile factory) 83; São Roque 74; São Vicente de Fora Monastery 78; shop front *90*; underground stations 225
Lisieux, France 56, 59
Liverpool 13, 84, 96, 98; St George's Hall *95*, 100
Lochgilphead, Scotland: Kilmory Castle 98
Loebnitz et Fils (Paris) 127
London 84; cinema *204*; The Circle *231*; City Club Cloakroom *120*; Debenham House *145*, 150, 153, 157; Harrods Meat Hall 150, *150*;

Leighton House *8*, *146*, 150; Michelin Building 163, *164*; Postman's Park *118*; St Anne's Flats, Doric Way *203*; St Thomas's Hospital (old) *114*; South Bank restaurant 211; Swan House, Chelsea 153; Swiss Cottage Square *229*; Tabbard Inn, Bedford Park 153; Temple Church 99, *99*; underground 225; Victoria & Albert Museum Grill Room 139, *148*; Westminster Abbey *12*, 16, *16*, 24, *24*, 99; Westminster Palace 19, 99, *100*, 102
Lorenzo da Viterbo 45
Los Angeles, Calif.: City Hall 189
Loudon, J. C.: *Encyclopaedia of Cottage, Farm and Villa Architecture* 98
Louisville, Ky: Seelbach Hotel 195–6, *196*
Low, John Gardner 170
Low Art Tile (Mass.) 168, *170, 170, 171*, 172
Ludowici Celadon (Ohio) 194
Lugwardine, Herts.: Penkelly House *121*
Lundberg, Anders 152
Lynam, Charles *118*, 123

MCDONALD, W. P. 175
McKim, Mead & White 182, 189
maiolica 41, 42, *42, 43*, 45, 59, 61, *61*
Makkum, Holland 64, 66, 91
Malibu Potteries (Calif.) *187*, 189
Malkin Edge & Co. (Staffordshire) 123
Malvern Priory, Worcester *30*
Mangualde, Portugal: Palácio dos Condes de Anadia *2*, 78
Mantua, Italy: Palace *43*, 45–6
Marazzi (Italian firm) *218*, 221, *221*
Marlborough Ceramics *218*, 221
Marly, Château de 59, 67
Masquelier (Lille factory) 59
Matisse, Henri 210, 211
Matos, Francisco de 74
Maw, George 121
Maw & Co. 102, 103, *114, 116, 118*, 121, 123, 138, 139, *141*, 153, *155*, 168, *205*, 221
Maypole Dairies *206*
Meaux Abbey, Yorkshire 21, *24*
Meissen State Porcelain Factory *211*
Memphis (design group) *218*
Mendes da Costa, Joseph *160*, 162, *162*
Mendini, Alessandro *199*, 218
Mercer, Henry Chapman *167*, 172, 176–7, *177, 178*, 192 (*see also* Moravian Pottery and Tile Works)
Mettlach, Germany 123
Milan: La Torre Arcobaleno *221*
Millán, Pedro 50, *55*

Minton, Herbert 98, 99, 100, 136
Minton & Co. *95*, 98, *98, 99*, 100, 103, 121, 138
Minton Art Pottery Studio *148*
Minton Hollins & Co. *95*, 110, 112, 123, 136, 139, 168, 200
Mintons China Works *102, 105, 113, 137, 138*, 139
Miró, Joan 210, 213, *215*
Modernism 13, 199, 203, 208, 210, 216
Mondrian, Piet 203, 216
Montmorency, Anne de 56, *56*
Moorish tiles 30–31, *31, 32, 33, 34*
Moravian Pottery and Tile Works (Penn) *167*, 176–7, *177, 178*, 190, 191, 195, *195*, 196
Morbihan, France: Château de Suscinio 27
Morgan (Matt) Art Pottery (Cincinnati) 182
Morgan, William De *see* De Morgan, William
Morisseau, Jean-Jacques 225, 229
Morot, Daniel 67
Morris, William 13, 105, 138, 141–2, *142, 143*, 145
Morris, Marshall, Faulkner & Co. 91, 141, *141*, 142, *142, 143*, 153
Mortellito, Domenico 185
Mosaic Tile Co. (USA) 168, 170
Moscow: Bolshoi Theatre 124
'Mudejar' style 31, *31, 32, 36*
Mueller, Emile 195
Mueller, Herman Carl 170, 172, 182, 185, 192
Mueller Mosiac Tile Co. (NJ) 182, *182*, 185, 196
Muller, J. S. 96

NAFELS, SWITZERLAND: Freuler Palace 85
Naples, Italy: S. Chiara (garden) *46*; S. Giovanni a Carbonara 45
Neatby, William J. 138, 150, *150*
Nemo, Nino 6
New Castle Delft (Britain) 221
Newport, IOW: Shide House *84*
New York: American Encaustic Tile Co. Building *192*, 194; Cathedral of St John the Divine 176; Chapel at West Point 177; Gainsborough Studios 190, *190*; Gramercy Park 194; Madison Square Presbyterian Church 189; 135 East 19th St *167*, 194; 139 East 19th St 194; 241 West 108th St 190–91; 730 Riverside Drive 194; 780 Riverside Drive 194, 195, *195*; Shattuck Building 192; subway 175, *175*, 176, *182*, 185, 192, 196; 780 West End Ave. 195, *195*; Vanderbilt Hotel 196
Nichols, Maria Longworth 172, 174, *174*
Niculoso, Francisco 46, 47, *47*, 50, 55
Nogueira, Rolando Sá 213, 225

Nolla, Miguel 132
Noordwijkerhout, Holland: 'De Vonk' *202*, 203
Norddeutsche Steingutfabrik (Grohn) 124
Norfolk, England 29, 84; Oxburgh Hall *117*; Wolferton Royal station urinal *120*
Nuremberg, Germany 85–6; underground *233*

OAKLAND, CALIF.: Paramount Theater *188*, 189
Oberwesel-am-Rhein, Germany: Schloss Schönburg chapel 28
Oeiras, Portugal: Palácio Pombal 83, *83*
O'Highway, Jan *228*
on-glaze decoration 59, 96, *96*, 142, *142*
Oort, Jan van 76, 78
Original Designers SR5 Studio (Milan) 221
Orvieto ware 42
Osborne, Arthur 170, *171*
Osborne House, IOW 100
Otterlo, Holland: Landhuis St Hubertus *160*, 162, *162*
Oud, Johannes 203

P & O LINE 150
Packwood House, Warwickshire *64*
Palgrave, Sir Francis 136
Palm Pottery (Britain) 221
Paris: Café Lipp *129*; Castel Bérenger 162–3, *163*; 106 rue du Château des Rentiers *231*; rue Franklin flats 163; Saint-Denis *22*; UNESCO 213, *215*
Pasadena, Calif.: Blacker House 194; Culbertson House 182, 194; Gamble House 194
Pas-de-Calais, France 16, 59
Pasmore, Victor 210, 211
Passenger, Charles and Fred 145
Passoles, Lorenzo *55*
pearlware 98
Penrhos, Anglesey: The Tower *110*
Perret, Auguste 152, 162, 163, 191
Perry, Mary Chase 172, 177, *181*, 182
Petrus Christus: *The Fountain of Life* 38
Pewabic Pottery, Detroit 177, *181*, 182, 194
Pewabic Society, Inc. 182
Pfau, Hans, II 85
Pfau, Johann 87
Pfund, Paul and Friedrich 124
Philadelphia, Pa: Exhibition (1876) 167, 168; Jacob Reed's Sons Store 191
Photo Decorated Tile Co. *103*
photographic tiles 102, *103*
Picasso, Pablo 210
Piccolpasso 42, 59
Pickman (Seville firm) 132

Piet Hein (Delfshaven factory) 91
Pietro de Andrea 45
Pilkington Tiles 139, *139, 206,* 208, 221
Plainsboro, NJ: Walker–Gordon Plant 185
Plateelbakkerij Delft (Hilversum) *204*
Poitiers, France: Palais de Justice 38
Pomar, Júlio 225
Ponchon, France 88
Portland, Oregon: Portland Building *10*
Post-Modernism 13, *119,* 216, 225, 229
Potsdam, Germany: Schloss Caputh 71
Poynter, Sir Edward John 138, 139, *148*
Price & McLanahan (architects) 191
printing methods 100, 102; *see also* screen printing; transfer printing
Prosser, Richard 98, 100, *100*
Providential Tile Works (USA) 168, 170, *172*
public houses *107, 108*
Pugin, A. W. N. 98, 99, *99,* 100, *100, 117,* 138
Purbeck Decorative Tile Co. (Britain) 208, 210, *219*
Pyne, W. H.: *Microcosm* 136
pyrometers 103

QUELUZ, PORTUGAL: Palácio Nacional *80,* 83

RACKHAM, BERNARD *61*
railway stations *114, 120,* 129, 176, 208, *210; see also* underground stations
Rambouillet, Château de 67, *71*
Ramié, Georges 210
Ramsgate, England: The Grange *99*
Rastatt, Germany: Schloss Favorite 86
Ravesteyn factory (Utrecht) 91, 142
Regout, Alfred 129, 132
Renaissance, the 13, 38, 42, 45, *47*
Rhead, Frederick *192*
Rhead, Loiz *192*
Ricardo, Halsey 145, 152, 153, 157
Richards Tiles Ltd (Stoke-on-Trent) 200
Rindge, May K. 189
Robertson Art Tile Co. (USA) 168, 170
Rochdale: town hall 100
Rodriguez, Mensaque 132
Rome: Castel Sant' Angelo 45; Loggias of Raphael, Vatican *45;* underground *222*
Rookwood Pottery (Cincinnati) *174,* 174–5, *175, 176, 181,* 182,

195–6, *196*
Rossetti, Dante Gabriel 141, *142, 143*
Rotterdam 63, *66, 67, 67,* 71, *71,* 78, 91
Rouen, France: Notre-Dame-du-Parc 21
Rowe, William, *114*
Rozenburg (The Hague) 129
Ruskin, John 105; *The Stones of Venice* 141

SAARINEN, ELIEL 182
Sacavém factory (Lisbon) 88, 132
Sadler, John 96, *96*
Sainsbury's: 'Green Dragon' tiles *112*
Saint-Amand-les-Eaux, France 59, *59*
Saint-Cloud, France 59
Saint-Omer, France: Cathedral de Notre-Dame 16, *19;* St-Bertin Abbey *15*
Saint-Paul, France 88
St Petersburg: Menshikov Palace 72; Summer Palace 72
Saint-Pierre-sur-Dives Abbey, Normandy 24
San Simeon, Calif.: La Casa Grande *187*
Santa Ana factory (Seville) 47, 88, *206*
'Sarrazin, le' 38
Sarreguemines (French firm) 132
Saxon tiles 16, 19, *19*
Schillemans factory (Utrecht) 91
Schloss Nymphenburg, Germany *68,* 71
Schut, Peter 66
Scranton, Penn.: Lackawana station 176
screen-painting *208, 210, 218, 219*
Seddon, J. P. 138
Selby, England: New Inn *205*
Septfontaines, Luxemburg 123
Servais & Cie (Ehrang) 124
Seville, Spain 30, 31, 46, 47, 88, 208; Casa de Pilatos 47, *48, 49;* Omnium Sanctorum 31, *36;* Plaza de España (bench) *209;* Santa Paula *55;* Torre del Oro 31; *see also* Alcázar, the
Shaw, Henry: *Specimens of Tile Pavements* 155
Shaw, Norman 152, 153
Shaws of Darwen 229, *231*
Sherbourne St John, England: The Vyne 61, *61*
Sherwin & Cotton (Staffordshire) 123
shops *112,* 113, *113,* 200
Shrubb Hill station, Worcester *114*
Silva, Vieira da 225
Simpson (W. B.) & Sons 103, *137, 155*
Simpson, W. P. 110, 136
'slabbing' 200, 208
slip 19
Smith, John Moyr 102, *102,* 138,

139
smuigers 66
'socarrat' tiles 36, 38
Société Anonyme des Carrelages Céramique 128
Société Céramique (Maastricht) 129, 132
Solon, Leon *192*
Sottsass, Ettore *218, 219*
Spode, Josiah 98
Stabler, Harold 200
'stamp-on-slip' technique 21
Stevens, Alfred *95*
stone tiles, 13th-century 16, *19*
Store Kongensgade (Copenhagen) 87, *87*
stove tiles 85–6, *86*
Stratton, William Buck 182
Sturehollm, Sweden: stove tiles *86*
subways *see* underground stations
Sutton Place, Surrey 153

TABULETAS, FERREIRA DAS 90
Talavera de la Reina, Spain 50, 56, 88; Nuestra Señora del Prado *52, 53,* 56
Thomas, C. R. 189
Thomas, Mark Hartland 208
Thomson, Margaret *114*
Thonwerke ceramics factory (Baden) 152
Thornton Abbey, S. Humberside *24*
Tichelaar factory (Makkum) 66, 91
Tiffany & Co. *181*
tiles: dust-pressed 100, *100,* 103, *103,* 121, 124, 127, 129, 138, 139; encaustic 98, *98*–100, *100, 115, 116,* 121, *121, 123*–4, *127, 128, 129,* 138; inlaid *15, 19, 21, 24, 24, 27, 27, 28, 29, 30,* 99; mosaic (medieval) *15,* 16, 19–21, *20, 21, 22;* relief (medieval) *19, 28, 28*–9, *29;* Saxon 16, 19, *19;* stone (13th-c.) 16, *19;* stove 85–6, *86; see also* glazes; Moorish tiles; printing methods
Till, Reginald, *208,* 210
Tjallingii factory (Harlingen) 91
Toledo, Spain: Convento de la Concepcion *36;* station 208
Toorop, Jan *160, 161,* 162
transfer printing 13, 85, 96, *96,* 98, 102, *102,* 103, 132, *138,* 139
Trent Tile Co. (USA) 168, 170
Trenton, NJ: Crescent Temple *182,* 185; Kelsey Memorial Building 185
Tucson, Arizona: Pima County Courthouse 189

UNDERGLAZE PRINTING 96, 98, *100, 102*
underground stations *114, 175, 175,* 176, *182,* 185, 192, 196, *222,* 225, *233*

United States Encaustic Tile Co. 168
Utrecht, Holland 28, 63, 91

VALENCIA 37–8, *38,* 88; Fábrica de Conservas, Catarroja *206;* Mercado de Colón *206, 207;* tiles *36,* 38, 45, 132
Valentine, Uffington *192*
van Hulst (Harlingen) 88, 91, *92,* 161
Velde, Henri van de 162
Vence, France: Chapelle du Rosaire 211
Venedigen, Frans van 61
Vermeer, Jan: *A Young Woman Standing at a Virginal* 62
Versailles: Trianon de Porcelaine 59, *67*
Vicens, Manuel 157
Vickers, Squire J. 192
Vienna: 'Majolika Haus' 163, *164;* Postsparkassenamt 163
Villeroy & Boch (Germany) 123, *123,* 124, *124, 126, 127,* 229
Viollet-le-Duc, Eugène 12, *22*
Viterbo, Italy: S. Maria della Verità 45
Voysey, C. F. A. 138, 139, *139,* 150, *152*

WAGNER, OTTO 152, 163, *164*
Wamps (Lille factory) 59
Washington, DC: Shrine 182
Watkins, Lura: 'Low's Art Tiles' 172
Watkin's heat recorder 103
Watts, G. F. *118*
Webb, Philip 141, *142, 143*
Wedgwood, Josiah 85, 96, 98, 103
Wedgwood Pottery Co. 102, 121, *137,* 145
Wellington, C. A. 172
Wenger, A. F. (Stoke-on-Trent) 103
Wessel's Wandplatten Fabrik (Bonn) 124
Wilmslow, Cheshire: Pownall Hall *88*
Wilton, New Hampshire: Library 176
Windsor, England: Royal Dairy *110*
Wise, William 105, 110, 113, 138, *138,* 139
Wolff, Johann 87
Worcester Porcelain Co. 98–9, 121
Worthington, Joseph 121
WPA (Works Progress Administration) 185
Wright, Samuel 98

YORK, ENGLAND: All Saints Church *19;* Bar Convent *116;* Royal York Hotel *107*
Ysbrechtum, Holland: Epema State *92*

ZUNZ, JEAN *224*
Zwart, Piet 202